D1376201

Middlesex County College
Library
Edison, New Jersey 08817

YEAS AND NAYS:

NORMAL DECISION-MAKING IN THE U.S. HOUSE OF REPRESENTATIVES

YEAS AND NAYS:

NORMAL DECISION-MAKING IN THE U.S. HOUSE OF REPRESENTATIVES

DONALD R. MATTHEWS
University of Michigan

JAMES A. STIMSON
State University of New York at Buffalo

A Wiley-Interscience Publication

JOHN WILEY & SONS, New York • London • Sydney • Toronto

Copyright © 1975 by John Wiley & Sons, Inc.

All rights reserved. Published simultaneously in Canada.

No part of this book may be reproduced by any means,
nor transmitted, nor translated into a machine language
without the written permission of the publisher.

Library of Congress Cataloging in Publication Data:

Matthews, Donald R
    Yeas and nays: normal decision-making in the U.S.
House of Representatives.

    "A Wiley-Interscience publication."
    Includes index.
    1. United States. House—Voting. I. Stimson,
James A., joint author. II. Title.

JK1447.M38   328.73′07′75   75-16124
ISBN 0-471-57695-6

Printed in the United States of America

10 9 8 7 6 5 4 3 2 1

PREFACE

This is a book about how congressmen make up their minds. In the following pages we present a theory of decision-making, argue for its utility as a way of understanding the American Congress, and report our efforts to test this theory by means of computer simulation and personal interviews with members of the U.S. House of Representatives. On the whole our data support the theory. Thus what follows is a relatively straightforward and self-contained research report. It can and should be judged on its merits, without regard to how it came to be.

But books have histories, and this one has more than most. The actual processes of research bear little resemblance to the idealized prescriptions of methodology textbooks. And the intellectual context within which books are conceived, as well as the processes by which they are born, affects their ultimate content. Thus some history of this study may add texture to this account and help readers understand where this work fits into the growing stream of research on congressional decision-making.[1]

In a sense this book began one day in the fall of 1966 when the junior author, then a first-year graduate student at the University of North Carolina, reported to work for the senior author as a research assistant. But the beginning of our professional association—which quickly evolved from a master–apprentice relationship to a genuine collaboration—was not really the start of it all. For we began thinking about congressional decision-making on the basis of what was known at the time. In retrospect it is clear that the puzzle we worried over in late 1966 was how, if at all, three seemingly disparate research traditions related to one another.

The first of these was the post-World War II research on congressional behavior.[2] The senior author was one of the early contributors to this line of research and had even speculated in print some years before about the decision processes employed by congressmen.[3] These tentative ideas had not been followed up; the platoons of political scientists who journeyed to Capitol Hill in the 1950s and 1960s mostly ignored member decision processes in favor of sociologically oriented studies of congressional committees and leadership groups within the House and Senate. They assumed that the "real" decisions of the House and Senate were made early in the legislative process by the key actors they studied. They were not much concerned with how these decisions were diffused to the entire membership of Congress.

Another and much smaller group of congressional scholars—the roll-call vote analysts—*were* interested in the decisions of all members of Congress.[4] But these scholars, at least at the time we began this work, employed individualistic and psychological models which implicitly assumed that members' personal attitudes were the proximate cause of their roll-call votes. There was thus an intriguing contradiction within the congressional literature on how congressmen make up their minds. The well-established findings of those who studied key decision-makers were but little reflected in the models of those who studied the decisions of rank and file members.

The second research tradition that influenced us was decision theory. These ideas were not particularly new, but their implications for legislative decision-making had not yet been explored. The major exceptions were the recently published works of the incrementalists[5] and Wildavsky's application of the theory to the politics of budgeting.[6] But while these books led us to think about low-cost modes of decision, it was the writings of Herbert Simon, in print for a decade, that most profoundly affected our decision model.[7]

Simultaneous emersion in the lore of Capital Hill and in theories of choice under conditions of bounded rationality eventually led us to ask a question not seriously studied by legislative scholars before: How would a reasonable congressman decide how to vote on an issue about which he knew and cared very little? Most legislative research, to the extent that it considered decision-making at all, zeroed in on "important" issues. It assumed that "pressures" impinged on members—from constituencies, parties, colleagues, or their own personal preferences. But how do members decide when these conditions do not hold, when the only effective pressure is to make a decision for the public record? Cues from trusted colleagues who do care about the issue and hence are better informed struck us as a plausible minimum cost–maximum benefit decision strategy for such occasions. Obviously we did not "discover" cue-taking in 1966—casual references to such a process abound in the descriptive and historical literature on Congress. Rather we resurrected an old observation, refined it into a scientific concept, and found that it fit into a general body of theory about rational choice.

The third intellectual tradition that affected our thinking about congressional decision-making was computer simulation. Our decision to operationalize and test our theory by computer modeling was based in part on necessity (we did not have easy access to Capitol Hill at that time) and in part on happenstance (we both wanted to learn how to do it).[8] But the fact that we started with the computer—and were provided almost unlimited time on a very good third-generation machine—had implications we did not appreciate at the time. From the very beginning we never considered, because we did not have to consider, selecting roll calls for analysis. Instead of choosing a few votes that were visible, important, typical, or whatever, we simply did the easiest thing and studied all roll calls.[9] And this, in turn, reinforced our inclination to study the routine, typical, ordinary side of decision-making.

That we started with a computer model also led us to postulate extremely simple decision behavior, without concern for the predictive failure that might result. Unlike methods that require prior commitment to expensive and inflexible research designs—and thus lead to a "Let's cover all the bases" scholarly conservatism—the failure of a computer model is not to be feared.[10] When computer models do not predict well, the modeler shares his secret with a dumb machine.

In the ordinary course of events most early models probably fail. When they do, the researcher adds successive layers of refinement until the model works or finally proves its fruitlessness. Our model never did fail. From the very earliest runs it showed a level of predictive accuracy that exceeded any in our experience. That it did so well from the start accounts for the fact that some refinements we thought necessary at the outset (e.g., to incorporate constituency influence and the previous positions of members) were never undertaken. We learned with some surprise that the inclusion of such factors, which we had always known would be difficult, was *unnecessary* for the accurate prediction of member votes. What was unnecessary for prediction slowly became suspect as explanation.

Computer modeling about 100,000 individual decisions per run made it infeasible to determine operationally which decisions were of the high-stakes, high-information variety. We simulated them with all the rest. And when we did, we simulated all decisions with great accuracy.[11] Our theory applied only to a subset, the low-stakes, routine decisions. Because the model worked so well, we came gradually to believe that our subset was most of the whole set. What was originally for us an interesting aberration became "normal decision-making."

The first public presentation of our preliminary results was made at the Conference on Political Decision-Making at the University of Kentucky in April 1968. The feedback from this paper[12] convinced us of the need for an independent check on the validity of our model. The model measured cue-taking propensities, observed cue-giver positions, and predicted member votes. It *assumed* communication between cue-giver and cue-taker. This seemed a reasonable assumption to us because the structure of the roll-call vote situation made such communication easy and because the levels of agreement between cue-givers and cue-takers were too high to be explained without communication. Some of our professional audience were less persuaded by this argument than we. And the almost uncanny predictive power of the model caused us to worry about the possibility of spurious accuracy. Thus we came to the conclusion that we had to *demonstrate* cue-taking in Congress. The only convincing way to do that was to talk to the members of the House of Representatives themselves.

Thus in February 1969 we moved to Washington and started preparations for a program of interviews with members of the House. The structure of our interviews reflected the fact that we had already developed and tested our theory. We knew our model worked; we needed support for our explanation of why it worked. Some critics did not believe that congressmen *normally* knew so little about a vote that they would prefer a trusted colleague's evaluation to their own. Hence we needed from the mouths of congressmen an estimate of the frequency of low-stakes, low-information decision-making. Even more vitally, we needed to confront members point-blank with the question of how they handled such situations. These data requisites, along with an overriding concern for candor in member responses to potentially sensitive questions,[13] were the essential ingredients in the design of our interviews.

Our interviews with members of the House were completed in June 1969, and the long process of analyzing these new data was begun. That almost six years has elapsed since then means that this study was designed and essentially completed before most of the recent literature on congressional decision-making appeared in print. Some of this recent work supports our theory, and some is at least partially at odds with it. We have read it all but remain unmoved from our conclusions of 1966.

We have accumulated a sobering number and variety of debts since that day we began working together. Our biggest creditor is undoubtedly the University of North Carolina at Chapel Hill. Not only did its Department of Political Science provide a congenial and intellectually exciting environment for the early stages of this exploration, but the University's Institute for Research in the Social Sciences, Research Council, and National Science Foundation Center for Excellence Steering Committee also provided cash. The University's Computing Center and its affiliate, the Triangle Universities Computation Center, also allocated an exceptionally generous amount of computer time to this project.

Other institutions that supported our work at various times and in various ways were The Center for Advanced Study in the Behavioral Sciences (where the senior author developed some of the ideas with which we began); The Ford Foundation (which granted the senior author a faculty research fellowship); The Brookings Institution (which supplied office space and its good name in Washington); The Inter-University Consortium for Political Research and the Louis Harris Political Data Center (from whom we obtained the roll-call data); and both the Center for Political Studies of the Institute for Social Research, University of Michigan, and the State University of New York Foundation (which supported the final stages of manuscript preparation).

We are grateful to the Harvard University Press; Columbia University Press; The Brookings Institution; Little, Brown & Company; and the American Political Science Association for permitting us to quote or reprint extended passages in this book.

A number of individuals directly assisted us along the way. In Chapel Hill, William Reynolds taught us much of what we know about PL/1 programming, Mark Schneider and Harry S. McGaughey were diligent research assistants; in Washington, Luther P. Cochrane aided in interviewing while Dianne Stimson coordinated our Capital Hill interviews, assisted in research, and labored at the tedious task of transcribing interviews from tape to paper; in Buffalo, Richard Calder rendered able research assistance and Lorraine Belczak was a faultless typist.

John L. Sullivan, David M. Kovenock, Duncan MacRae, Jr., and W. Phillips Shively read and commented on portions of this manuscript; Richard F. Fenno and Edward G. Carmines read every line and commented on most. These readers have saved us from many egregious errors of fact and interpretation; those that remain should be attributed to the stubbornness of the authors.

Our final debt is to 100 members of the U.S. House of Representatives. They gave us their time, a precious commodity, without hope of personal gain. Sometimes their answers to our questions were potentially embarrassing, but they still gave them to scholars they did not know. Their tape-recorded remarks must go unattributed in this volume, but we have had warm memories of their names and faces as we wrote every page.

Thank you, thank you, each and every one.

DONALD R. MATTHEWS
JAMES A. STIMSON

Ann Arbor, Michigan
Buffalo, New York
July 1975

NOTES

1. Among the more notable works in this growing literature are the following: Cleo H. Cherryholmes and Michael J. Shapiro, *Representatives and Roll Calls* (Indianapolis: Bobbs-Merrill, 1969); John S. Jackson, "Statistical Models of Senate Roll Call Voting," *American Political Science Review,* Vol. 65 (1971), pp. 451–470; Aage R. Clausen, *How Congressmen Decide: A Policy Focus* (New York: St. Martin's, 1973); Herbert B. Asher, *Freshmen Representatives and the Learning of Voting Cues* (Beverly Hills and London: Sage Professional Paper in American Politics 04-003, 1973); John W. Kingdon, *Congressmen's Voting Decisions* (New York: Harper & Row, 1973); Morris P. Fiorina, *Representatives, Roll Calls and Constituencies* (Lexington, Massachusetts: D. C. Heath, 1974); and John S. Jackson, *Constituencies and Leaders in Congress* (Cambridge, Massachusetts: Harvard University Press, 1974).

2. A good survey and introduction to this literature is Robert L. Peabody's introduction to R. K. Huitt and R. L. Peabody, *Congress: Two Decades of Analysis* (New York: Harper & Row, 1969), pp. 3–73.

3. Donald R. Matthews, *U.S. Senators and Their World* (Chapel Hill: University of North Carolina Press, 1960), pp. 249.

4. Leading early examples of this approach are Duncan MacRae, Jr., *Dimensions of Congressional Voting* (Berkeley: University of California Press, 1958) and H. Douglas Price, "Are Southern Democrats Different? An Application of Scale Analysis to Senate Voting Patterns," in N. W. Polsby, R. A. Dentler, and P. A. Smith (eds.), *Politics and Social Life* (Boston: Houghton-Mifflin, 1963), pp. 740–756.

5. See particularly David Braybrooke and Charles E. Lindblom, *A Strategy of Decision* (New York: Free Press, 1963). The newness of incrementalist theory can be overstressed. Lindblom had presented a preliminary statement of the idea in "The Science of 'Muddling Through,'" *Public Administration Review*, Vol. 19 (1959), pp. 79–88.

6. Aaron Wildavsky, *The Politics of the Budgetary Process* (Boston: Little, Brown, 1964).

7. Herbert A. Simon, *Models of Man: Social and Rational* (New York: Wiley, 1955).

8. The Cherryholmes and Shipiro simulation was well underway at this time, but we were unaware of its existence until later.

9. By way of contrast, John Kingdon's ingenious research design could not be applied to decision-making on more than a few roll calls. Since selectivity was inescapable, he chose to confine his attention to highly visible, controversial, "big" votes. *Congressmen's Voting Decisions*, p. 16. His model therefore pertains to a different set of roll calls than ours.

10. Paul Diesing, *Patterns of Discovery in the Social Sciences* (Chicago: Aldine-Atherton, 1971), suggests that predictive failure is a desirable result in what he calls "formalist experiments."

11. See Donald R. Matthews and James A. Stimson, "Decision-Making by U.S. Representatives: A Preliminary Model," in S. Sidney Ulmer (ed.), *Political Decision-Making* (New York: Van Nostrand Reinhold, 1970), pp. 14–43, for an extended discussion of patterns of predictive error.

12. *Ibid.* Other progress reports made along the way include Matthews and Stimson, "The Decision-Making Approach to the Study of Legislative Behavior," presented at the Sixty-Fifth Annual Meeting of the American Political Science Association, September, 1969; Matthews and Stimson, "Cue-Taking by Congressmen: A Model and a Computer Simulation," presented at the Conference on the Use of Quantitative Methods in the Study of the History of Legislative Behavior, University of Iowa, March 1972; Stimson, "The Diffusion of Evaluations: Patterns of Cue-Taking in the United States House of Representatives," unpublished Doctoral Dissertation, University of North Carolina, 1970; and Stimson, "Five Propositions About Congressional Decision-Making: An Examination of Behavioral Inferences from Computer Simulation," *Political Methodology*, Vol. 2 (1975), in press.

13. The interview proved less sensitive for most respondents than we had expected.

CONTENTS

YEAS AND NAYS:

NORMAL DECISION-MAKING IN THE U.S. HOUSE OF REPRESENTATIVES

CHAPTER ONE

INTRODUCTION

> Each House shall keep a Journal of its Proceedings, and from time to
> time publish the same, excepting such parts as may in their Judgment
> require Secrecy; and the Yeas and Nays of the Members of either House
> on any question shall, at the Desire of one fifth of those Present, be
> entered on the Journal.
> United States Constitution, Article I, Section 5

Over 200 times a year a chattering, backslapping group of men and
women spills onto the floor of the House. The mob swells, recruiting
new members from cloakrooms and offices. It surges one way and then
the other across the floor. Finally, it ebbs out the doorways—leaving
behind order, quiet, and an authoritative decision of the House.
Nearly two centuries after the solemn stipulation of Article I, the roll-
call vote is a common—if not altogether comforting—sight in the U.S.
House of Representatives.

If some of the procedure for the calling of the Yeas and Nays has
changed, the Founders' intent is intact. The calling of the roll is no
longer a singsong chant of question and answer. Instead of shouted
Ayes's and No's dancing lights on a wall scoreboard record members'

positions. The Yeas and Nays remain, as the Founders intended, public affirmations of support or opposition for the acts of a republican government.

This book is about congressional decision-making, particularly that which is reflected in roll-call votes. More particularly it is about *normal* decision-making. It is about those hundreds of decisions that dispense billions of dollars, constitute most of the sum total of the policy of the United States Government, and yet attract little public notice.

This book is about the apparent chaos of congressional decision-making and its underlying order. It is about the psychology of decision, about the economy of decision, and ultimately its rationality. Its focus is the individual member decision, particularly the routine and the typical. Its explanatory problem is this: How do men blessed with only human capability make large numbers of apparently rational decisions, faced with constraints that defy rationality?

WHY STUDY HOUSE ROLL CALLS?

Some would deny that this is a subject worthy of serious investigation. Some argue that the Congress, especially the House of Representatives, has precious little effect on the nation's policies. Others hold that roll-call votes in the House are not very important, that the "real" decisions of the House of Representatives are not made on its floor. If either of these allegations were true, there would be little point in reading a book—or writing one—on roll-call voting by congressmen. Let us examine each of those allegations in turn.

Is the House of Representatives Powerless?

"Every day in every way the power of the Congress is being diluted" lamented a senior member of the House of Representatives a few years ago.[1] Most of his colleagues, most political journalists, and most professional students of Congress agree.[2]

The main burden of the case for the powerlessness of Congress is carried by the assertion that it has lost the initiative to the President and the bureaucracy in making legislation.[3] "If Congress legislates, it subordinates itself to the President," Samuel Huntington writes in an influential essay. "If it refuses to legislate, it alienates itself from public opinion. Congress can assert its power or it can pass laws; but it cannot do both."[4]

There is an element of truth in this view: the twentieth century has not been kind to legislatures. Unable to deal effectively with the magnitude and complexity of contemporary problems, most national legislatures in the West have been reduced to little more than debating societies. But Congress has been something of an exception to this rule.

True, Congress rarely acts on important matters without an Administration bill. The President's policy program largely sets the legislative agenda.[5] But this does not mean that members of Congress play no role in policy initiative. As Nelson Polsby writes:[6]

> How are policies initiated in the American political system? The process is by no means uniform, or clear. It is certainly not generally true that policy innovation begins with a presidential message to Congress. For behind each presidential message lurk months of man-hours of work and sometimes years of advocacy and controversy. The two great fountainheads of policy seem to be: (1) sudden demands upon government that spur bureaucrats to ad-hoc problem solving that ultimately has to be codified or rationalized as "policy;" and (2) a longer range build-up in the society of some demand upon the government where the formulation of a "solution" may first be made by a professor, or by technical support personnel attached to an interest group, or by a government "expert." On rare occasions, experts attached to a Congressional committee will initiate policy. More often, I think, Congress is in on the beginning of a policy innovation because it provides the first sympathetic ear for an innovation concocted by outside experts.

One of the few efforts to probe the genesis of recent public policies is James L. Sundquist's important study of domestic policy formulation during the Eisenhower, Kennedy, and Johnson years.[7] He finds not one but two systems of policy initiative—one executive, the other congressional—with different attributes and strengths and weaknesses. During the slack Eisenhower years, activist-liberal Democrats in Congress formulated and popularized a set of domestic policies which they then lobbied the Kennedy and Johnson Administrations to accept as their own.[8]

> In the fields of air and water pollution, in particular, Congress demonstrated that it had not lost its capacity to initiate where the administration, for one reason or another, lagged. In these areas, it was Congress that led and the administration that followed. Moreover, on many measures where the President led, the contribution of Congress was still substantial. Major sections of the Civil Rights Act of 1964 and the medicare act were of legislative origin. Congress initiated the grant features of the college assistance legislation. The Johnson proposal for assistance to elementary and secondary education was built around an approach that in its initial form at least, can be credited to Senator Morse. The Accelerated Public Works Act and the Manpower Development and Training Act were recast by Congress. Only on a minority of the measures enacted did Congress relinquish wholly the legislative role. And in 1966, as the President and his administration became steadily more preoccupied with the war in Vietnam and the budget stringency brought on by that conflict, the initiative for devising new and effective measures to meet the crisis in the Negro ghettos appeared to be moving from the executive branch to activists on Capitol Hill.[9]

Moreover, those who seek new legislation must constantly anticipate what Congress will accept as well as what the President will buy—and these are frequently as different as are the constituencies to which the President and leading congressional figures respond most easily. Initiative and power are not the same thing in a game in which each player must anticipate the actions of the other.[10] He who conceives a bill may be less important in shaping its content then those who have to accept his handiwork. Thus ". . . Congress maintain(s) a large measure of control over what goes into a bill and what happens to it, regardless of its origins."[11]

Twentieth-century government is executive-centered government. But the House and Senate are far from being impotent or irrelevant. Their actions (and inactions) shape public policy. Ask any president—or bureau chief.

Are House Roll Calls Meaningless?

Another cliché about the House of Representatives holds that "real" decisions are not made in public on the floor: roll-call votes merely ratify decisions made by standing committees in secret or by nonrecorded votes cast in the Committee of the Whole. There is well-worn truth to this view. But this does not mean that roll calls have little impact on public policy or are unworthy of study by those seeking to understand how public policy is made.

Most legislative proposals are referred to standing committees and are never heard of again. In recent Congresses 10,000 to 20,000 bills and resolutions have been introduced; only about 2,000 per Congress were reported out by one of the House committees (see Table 1-1). Thus 80 to 90 percent of all legislative proposals suffer a silent death in House committee rooms. This is a vast, basically negative, exercise of power over public policy that an analysis of roll-call votes fails to include.

But there are numerous checks and restraints on its arbitrary use on important matters. Committees may be "discharged" by means of a petition signed by a majority of House members that brings a bill to the floor despite committee inaction. The fact that discharge petitions are rarely attempted and almost never succeed does not detract from the threat they pose to any committee wishing to kill a proposal that a solid majority of the House feels is important and meritorious.[12] Most committees prefer to report a bill than to be bypassed.

The openness and decentralization of Congress provide an even more important inhibition to committees killing important legislative proposals without benefit of public debate and voting. As Sundquist writes:

> A good idea initiated on Capitol Hill cannot be killed by the judgment, or the whim, of any individual; it is in the public domain, it will gain support on its merits through public awareness and discussion, and if a committee chairman refuses to hold hearings, there are many safety valves: a second house, other committees that may assert jurisdiction, the opportunity to initiate action on the Senate floor. Granted, a Howard Smith [former Chairman of the House Rules Committee] may exercise

great obstructive power as an individual. . . . [But] the power granted him can be withdrawn by the body granting it.[13]

This, of course, is exactly what happened to "Judge" Smith in 1961. Frustrated by the Rules Committee's unwillingness to bring liberal legislation to the floor—the Rules Committee must grant a special rule before most important committee-approved bills can come to

TABLE 1-1   NUMBER OF BILLS AND RESOLUTIONS INTRODUCED IN THE U.S. HOUSE OF REPRESENTATIVES AND NUMBER REPORTED BY STANDING COMMITTEE, 1947–1972

Congress and Years	Number of Bills and Resolutions Introduced in House	Number of Bills and Resolutions Reported by House Committees	Percent Reported of All Bills and Resolutions Introduced
93rd, 1973–74	21,095	1333	6
92nd, 1971–72	20,458	1401	7
91st, 1969–70	23,575	1542	7
90th, 1967–68	24,227	1745	7
89th, 1965–66	21,999	2062	9
88th, 1963–64	15,299	1742	11
87th, 1961–62	15,751	2302	15
86th, 1959–60	15,506	1994	13
85th, 1957–58	15,660	2450	16
84th, 1955–56	14,104	2698	19
83rd, 1953–54	11,864	2442	21
82nd, 1951–52	10,055	2297	23
81st, 1949–50	11,695	2924	25
80th, 1947–48	8,561	2180	25

Sources: *Congressional Record*, November 8, 1972 (p. D1227); January 2, 1971 (p. D739); October 14, 1968 (p. D483); October 22, 1966 (p. D604); October 1, 1964 (p. D506); October 13, 1962 (p. D625); September 1, 1960 (p. D492); August 23, 1958 (p. D610); July 27, 1956 (p. D642); December 2, 1954 (p. D741); July 7, 1952 (p. D501); January 2, 1951 (p. D759); December 31, 1948 (p. D537), January 10, 1975 (p. D1427).

the floor—a majority of the House voted to enlarge the Rules Committee from 12 to 15 members. "By adding two pro-Administration Democrats and only one Republican to a committee previously dominated by two conservative Democrats and four Republican minority members, a six-to-six stalemate was converted to an eight-to-seven majority generally sympathetic to the needs of the Democratic leadership."[14] Since that time, the obstructive power of the Rules Committee has been little exercised. Even before the Committee was "packed," Judge Smith and his conservative colleagues were rarely able to kill legislation in the face of a solid House majority desiring the contrary.[15]

Thus most legislative proposals killed by House committees are too weak to put up much of a fight. Most major bills enjoying a substantial popular and congressional support get to the floor—often, to be sure, bearing deep scars from the sometimes lengthy committee struggle. In recent years, the authoritative *Congressional Quarterly Almanac* has compiled lists of "major" legislative proposals introduced in each Congress: over the last decade, 82 percent of these have been reported and were debated and voted up or down on the floor (see Table 1-2). This committee survival rate is in marked contrast to the 10 to 20 percent figure for *all* bills and resolutions, big and small.

The lion's share of legislation that passes the House is agreed to by unanimous consent. Most private bills (which benefit particular named individuals) and many public bills and resolutions are read by the clerk and "if the chair hears no objection" are passed after little or no discussion. Obviously bills passed in this way have generated no controversy and are of little general importance.[16]

More controversial matters are ordinarily handled in two stages. First, the bill is considered by "The Committee of the Whole House on the State of the Union." The Speaker relinquishes his chair to another member, the mace is removed from the dais, and the quorum necessary to conduct business is reduced to 100 (from 218, half the House membership). It is in this relatively informal atmosphere that the general debate on the bill is conducted and amendments voted up or down.

TABLE 1-2   NUMBER AND PERCENT OF "MAJOR" PROPOSALS REPORTED
             BY COMMITTEES OF U.S. HOUSE, 1957–72

Congress and Years	Number of "Major" Proposals According to C.Q. Almanac	Number of "Major" Proposals Reported by Committees	Percent of "Major" Proposals Reported
93rd, 1973–74	17	15	88
92nd, 1971–72	25	19	76
91st, 1969–70	26	22	85
90th, 1967–68	21	19	91
89th, 1965–66	25	19	76
88th, 1963–64	25	18	72
87th, 1961–62	25	22	88
86th, 1959–60	26	20	77
85th, 1957–58	26	23	89
Total	216	177	82

Sources: *Congressional Quarterly Almanac*, Vol. XXVIII (1972), p. 10; Vol. XXVI (1970), p. 72; Vol. XXIV (1968), p. 68; Vol. XXII (1966), p. 68; Vol. XX (1964), p. 62; *Congressional Quarterly Weekly Reports*, October 19, 1962; September 23, 1960; August, 29, 1958, January 4, 1975.

Voting in the Committee of the Whole takes one of three forms: a voice vote, a division (members stand to be counted by the Speaker), or a teller vote (members walk up the center aisle to be counted by tellers). These different voting procedures are regularly used in combination. After an initial voice vote, any single member may request a division—and, of course, members on the losing side exercise this right frequently. If this division is relatively close, a demand for tellers is usually made. When this demand is supported by 20 members, the Speaker appoints two tellers, a single bell rings, and the members march down the center aisle to be counted. Before 1971 votes in the Committee of the Whole were not recorded; the presiding officer merely announced the total number of ayes and noes cast; no tally was kept of the votes of individual members. The Legislative Reorganization Act of 1970 authorized recorded teller votes at the request of 20 members.

Critical decisions about proposed amendments to major legislation are often made by only a fraction of the House membership in the Committee of the Whole. Amendments adopted by the Committee of the Whole are subject to the vote of the House when the bill is presented from the Committee of the Whole to the House for final approval. But amendments *defeated* in Committee of the Whole are not reported and seldom can be reconsidered by the House at a later point.[17] These defeated amendments—and most proposed amendments are defeated—are a significant category of major policy decisions that are made without benefit of roll-call voting.

But not all such decisions escape, thereby, the purview of this study. Attendance at sessions of the Committee of the Whole is spotty at best. Even with its relaxed quorum requirement, the committee often operates with less than 100 members on the floor. Whenever less than a quorum votes on a division or teller vote, any member may object, and an "automatic" roll call occurs—a quorum call in which members, rather than answering "present," vote "aye" or "nay" on the amendment at issue. This situation occurs frequently enough to give students of House roll calls a number of recorded votes on defeated amendments to analyze.

Once all amendments have been dispensed with, the Committee of the Whole reports back to the House, the Speaker and the mace reappear, and a quorum becomes 218 members once again. At this point the amendments adopted by the Committee of the Whole are voted upon again, usually *en bloc* in order to save time, but important and controversial amendments can be voted on one at a time if such a demand is made by a single member. Once the amendments have been voted up or down, motions to recommit are in order and, when that fails, a vote on final passage.

Roll-call votes are not required at any of these points; however, a demand supported by one-fifth of the members (87) necessitates a roll call. Thus roll calls tend to occur on relatively controversial matters—when the losers on a prior division or teller vote hope that better attendance and a recorded vote may change the result—or on matters which, for a variety of reasons, at least one-fifth of the members wish to be recorded. The desire to be publicly recorded foursquare in favor of God, country, and motherhood is strong among elective politicians and leads to a number of nearly unanimous "Hurrah Votes." But a successful demand for a roll call usually means that at least 87 members feel that the issue is important enough to be worth an investment of a half-hour of their precious time.

This brief excursion into House procedures and voting rules demonstrates, we believe, that roll calls usually are taken on relatively major and relatively controversial issues. Not all roll calls are "important" or are on subjects about which the House is closely divided, but few major decisions are made without benefit of at least one recorded vote.

Are these roll-call votes merely a *pro forma* "ratification" of decisions made earlier in the complex and lengthy legislative process? Certainly committee recommendations usually carry the day on the House floor. Few amendments are proposed to committee-approved bills; relatively few of these are accepted—especially when the committees are united in opposition.[18] And yet the opportunity to challenge committee decisions does exist and—no matter how uneven the contest usually is—this opportunity is regularly exercised. In "marking up" bills for floor presentation, committee members must anticipate what their colleagues not on the committee will support. The absence of floor amendments and the regular defeat of those amendments that are introduced indicate, more than anything else, that the committees are generally successful in anticipating the preferences of a majority of the House. Floor votes are thus profoundly affected by what has transpired earlier in the legislative process; but the early stages of the legislative process are heavily shaped by the anticipation of floor votes as well. Fenno has described this interaction well:[19]

> An Appropriations Committee decision, whatever it may be and however it may have been arrived at, is not an authoritative decision of

the House of Representatives. It is but a recommendation submitted to members of the parent chamber for their approval. Only the House, acting as a body and in accordance with certain prescribed procedures, can pass an appropriation bill and send that bill on to the Senate. Once the Committee has made its recommendations, therefore, its members must turn to the task of winning support for these decisions among their House colleagues. It is, of course, no new concern for committee members. They know that house member support is, for the most part, won or lost well in advance of any debate and decision on the floor. And they remain continuously attentive and responsible to Member expectations and images throughout their deliberations. Still, decision-making on the House floor is not the same as decision-making inside the Appropriations Committee. And no matter how much advance consideration may have been given to the desires of the "the House," anticipation is not the same as a direct confrontation. The House floor is a special context.

It is decision-making within this "special context" that concerns us in this book.

A Note on Research Strategy

Even though roll-call votes in the House are neither trivial nor foreordained they still may not merit an investment of the limited resources available for legislative research. Could not greater payoffs be expected from studies of other aspects of legislative behavior, other phases of the legislative process? We think not.[20]

If one accepts the view, as we do, that the ultimate purpose of legislative research is to explain the policy outputs of legislative bodies such as the House of Representatives, then the most sensible strategy for research would seem to be to focus on the outputs of legislatures. Then, the researcher's task is to discover the antecedent "causes" of these outputs. Our strategy is to focus attention on the final stages of decision—on the individual choice processes before the roll-call vote is cast—and then to search for "causes" in the chain of events preceding the vote.[21] This strategy is comparable to that followed by the authors of *The American Voter* who, by focusing on the processes immediately preceding the voter's decision, were able to revolutionize the study of electoral behavior.[22] We hope that by focusing our research on events proximate to decision-making we may achieve a breakthrough in the study of legislative behavior as well. Certainly it is worth a try.

THE APPROACH AND THE DATA

The explicit focus of this study is the *process* by which individual members make decisions. What is going on in members' heads as they make their decisions is our concern. There are of course multiple decision processes, but we argue that one, to be called "cue-taking,"[23] is the *normal* process, the one employed by most members on most votes. Cue-taking, as we use the concept, means more than simple interpersonal influence. It is a self-conscious decision strategy well suited to the special decision situation of members of Congress.

To make this argument we discuss (in Chapter 2) the constraints imposed on member decision-making by the number, scope, and technical complexity of required decisions. Various decision shortcuts are examined as possible solutions to this decision overload.

In Chapter 3 our theory of cue-taking is developed in a more formal fashion. The logic of specialization, the relative insignificance of roll-call votes for electoral aspirations, and the compelling need for decision economy are shown to combine to make cue-taking a near ideal solution to a difficult problem.

The incidence of cue-taking and patterns of cue diffusion are, respectively, the subjects of Chapters 4 and 5, where we fill in some of the more important details of our theory of cue-talking.

In Chapter 6 we discuss an operational model of cue-taking, a computer simulation of individual roll-call decision-making. The simulation results provide a more formal perspective on many of the same questions discussed in earlier chapters.

We switch from the individual to the aggregate decision level in the final chapter, examining the impact of the cue-giving process on decisions of the House, and raising some familiar normative questions from our rather different theoretical perspective.

Throughout we rely on two distinct data sets. First, we make heavy use of the results of 100 structured interviews conducted with a random sample of House members during the late winter and spring of 1969. A copy of the questionnaire, plus full descriptions of our sampling and interviewing procedures may be found in Appendixes A and B. Second, our computer simulation beginning with the published record of all roll calls cast by members from 1965 to 1969[24] generates "predicted" (actually, postdicted) votes for all members on all issues. By comparing these predictions with actual behavior we can arrive at some conclusions about the validity of the model and its utility for analytical purposes. The more technical aspects of the computer simulation are described in Appendix C.

NOTES

1. Congressman F. Edward Herbert (D., La.) in *The Congress and America's Future*, Report of the Seventh Air Force Academy Assembly (Colorado Springs, Colorado: U.S. Air Force Academy, 1965), p. 22.

2. See R. H. Davidson, D. M. Kovenock, and M. K. O'Leary, *Congress in Crisis: Politics and Congressional Reform* (Belmont, Calif.: Wadsworth, 1966), Chapters 2 and 3 for the presentation of systematic data on the attitudes towards Congress of these groups.

3. See L. Chamberlain, *The President, Congress and Legislation* (New York: Columbia University Press, 1946) for the seminal work; J. A. Robinson, *Congress and Foreign Policy Making* (Homewood, Ill.: The Dorsey Press, rev. ed., 1967), especially pp. 1–69, is a more recent work concerned with policy initiatives in foreign policy.

4. "Congressional Responses to the Twentieth Century," in D. B. Truman (ed.), *The Congress and America's Future* (Englewood Cliffs, N.J.: Prentice-Hall, 1965), p. 6.

5. See R. E. Neustadt, "Presidency and Legislation: The Growth of Central Clearance," *American Political Science Review*, Vol. 48 (1954), pp. 641–71 and "Presidency and Legislation: Planning the President's Program," *ibid.*, Vol. 49 (1955), pp. 980–1021; D. B. Truman, *The Congressional Party* (New York: Wiley, 1959), especially Chapters 1 and 8.

6. "Policy Analysis and Congress," *Public Policy*, Vol. 18 (1969), p. 66.

7. James L. Sundquist, *Politics and Policy: The Eisenhower, Kennedy and Johnson Years* (Washington, D.C.: The Brookings Institution, 1968).

8. *Ibid.*, p. 489ff.

9. *Ibid.*, p. 495.

10. C. J. Friedrich, *Constitutional Government and Politics* (New York: Harper Brothers, 1937) first formulated this "rule of anticipated reactions" so often ignored in discussions of presidential-congressional initiatives.

11. K. R. Huitt, "Congress, The Durable Partner" in E. Franke (ed.), *Lawmakers in a Changing World* (Englewood Cliffs, N.J.: Prentice-Hall, 1966), p. 17.

12. The best introduction to House procedures is L. A. Froman, Jr., *The Congressional Process* (Boston: Little, Brown, 1967). The discharge rule is discussed on pp. 90–93. Other ways of bypassing legislative committees exist, see Chapter 5. J. A. Robinson, *The House Rules Committee* (Indianapolis: Bobbs-Merrill, 1963), p. 33, writes: "Between 1937 and 1958 more than two hundred Discharge Petitions were filed, but only twenty-one (an average of one a session) obtained the requisite number of signatures to be placed on the Discharge Calendar. Thirteen of these passed the House, but only one (the Wage and Hour Act of 1938) also received both Senatorial and Presidential support, thus becoming law."

13. Sundquist, *op. cit.*, pp. 492–3.

14. R. L. Peabody, "The Enlarged Rules Committee," in R. L. Peabody and N. Polsby (eds.), *New Perspectives on the House of Representatives* (Chicago: Rand McNally, 1963), pp. 129–30. See also M. C. Cummings, Jr., and R. L. Peabody, "The Decision to Enlarge the Committee on Rules: An Analysis of the 1961 Vote," pp. 167–94 in the same volume.

15. The basic argument about the Rules Committee is over what kind of majority the committee should represent and respond to: reformers have argued that the committee should be an agent of the *majority party* and its leadership; proponents of the *status quo* have argued that the committee should remain independent of the majority party leadership and represent the conservative House majority of Southern Democrats and Republicans. See Robinson, *op. cit.*, for a full discussion.

16. See L. A. Froman, *The Congressional Process: Strategies, Rules and Procedures* (Boston: Little, Brown, 1967), Chapter 4 for more detail on House procedures than is appropriate here.

17. See Froman, *op. cit.*, pp. 83–85.

18. See R. F. Fenno, Jr., *The Power of the Purse* (Boston: Little, Brown, 1966), Chapter 9 for the best discussion of committee-House relationships now available. During the period of his study, the powerful House Appropriations Committee was successful in defeating 77 percent of all floor amendments to which it was opposed (p. 453). This is an impressive batting average. Yet given the numerous advantages the Committee possesses in a floor fight the fact that the challenges of the committee are successful over 20 percent of the time is a noteworthy achievement as well.

19. Fenno, *Op. cit.*, p. 414.

20. For a more extended presentation of the following argument, see D. R. Matthews and J. A. Stimson, "The Decision-Making Approach to the Study of Legislative Behavior: The Example of the U.S. House of Representatives," a paper delivered at the American Political Science Association Annual Meeting, September 6–9, 1969 (mimeographed).

21. For similar orientations to the strategy of studying decision strategies see John W. Kingdon, *Congressmen's Voting Decisions* (New York: Harper & Row, 1973); and Cleo Cherryholmes and Michael Shapiro, *Representatives and Roll Calls* (Indianapolis: Bobbs-Merrill, 1969).

22. Angus Campbell, Phillip Converse, Warren Miller, and Donald Stokes, *The American Voter* (New York: Wiley, 1960).

23. It is appropriate to point out here that neither the idea of cue-taking nor the terminology are novel. The notion of cue-taking, under various labels, abounds in writings of observers of Congress. What is new here is the assertion that it is the *normal* decision process, to which others are exceptions.

24. We have also simulated some earlier sessions with computer models which, though similar, are not exactly comparable to the one presented here. See D. R. Matthews and J. A. Stimson, "Decision-Making by U.S. Representatives: A Preliminary Model," in S. Sidney Ulmer (ed.), *Political Decision-Making* (New York: Van Nostrand Reinhold, 1970), pp. 14–43.

CHAPTER TWO

DECISIONS ON THE FLOOR: CONSTRAINTS AND PARTIAL SOLUTIONS

On November 5, 1969, the Yeas and Nays were ordered on a motion to recommit HR6678 to the Committee on Banking and Currency. The motion failed by a vote of 124 to 245, and the subsequent vote on final passage of the bill was nearly unanimous.[1] An amendment to the Bank Holding Company Act of 1956, HR6678 was a fairly "typical" piece of legislation. Although it had been reported in the press, few voters had ever heard of the bill, or ever would. It was, however, of considerable interest to the financial community. While Democratic and Republican members of the House often were on opposite sides of the issue, it was not one of those conflicts in which the parties took sharply defined opposing positions.

HR6678 was designed to include so-called "one-bank holding companies" under the same federal regulations that had previously covered only holding companies controlling several banks. The clear intent was to keep banks out of nonbanking commercial enterprises and the latter out of banking; its proponents believed that the inclu-

16

sion of banks in conglomerate and other holding companies resulted in an excessive concentration of economic power. The bill, which consisted of three amendments to existing legislation, was expressed in relatively simple language, as legislation goes. But the simplicity of language covered up a subject matter of great complexity. A full understanding of the bill required substantial familiarity with theoretical economics, the recent history of the American economy, the legislative history of banking regulation, and the technical complexities of the banking industry. The adept congressman would also want to know which companies in his district would be affected, how much, and what implications a pro or con position on the bill might have for his political future.

The complexity of the subject matter kept most members of the House silent during debate in the Committee of the Whole. Indeed most of them were not on the House floor at all—the proceedings were interrupted once for lack of the necessary 100-member quorum. As is usually the case, debate was dominated by members of the committee reporting the bill, Banking and Currency in this case.

All this might suggest that the matter was one of little importance. Nothing could be further from the truth. The terms of this act would fundamentally alter the American economy in the years to come—on this everyone who participated in the debate agreed. The bill was the result of four months of committee hearings and additional months of staff work. Several executive agencies had provided volumes of detailed information, and lobbyists were active on both sides.

THE PROBLEM

It is instructive to look at the context within which members of the House decided how to cast their roll-call votes on this and similar issues.

The Number of Decisions

One aspect of this context is the sheer number of voting decisions that have to be made.

I have to vote on 150 different kinds of things every year—foreign aid,
science, space, technical problems, and the Merchant Marine, and Lord
knows what else. I can't possibly become an expert in all of these fields.[2]

Thus does a member of Congress describe the formidable decision-
making task he and his colleagues face. The recommittal motion on
HR6678 was only one of 177 recorded roll-call votes they were expected to cast in 1969 (the First Session of the Ninety-first Congress).
And there has been a trend toward more and more roll-call votes in
the House for over a decade.[3]

When nonrecorded floor votes are added—to say nothing of the
many decisions congressmen must make in committee, in their offices,
and elsewhere—it is apparent that members are required to make an
unusually large number of decisions.

The Scope of Decisions

The subject matter of these decisions is as varied as twentieth century
America is complex. On the day the House passed HR6678, members
also discussed on the floor (in one form or another) national egg inspection, aircraft cost overruns, school desegregation, the war in
Vietnam, defense appropriations, food stamps, office equipment for
members of the House, the poverty program, draft reform, the problems of air travel and the Supersonic Transport, crime, education,
problems of the District of Columbia, consumer protection, and rural
electrification.[4] The scope of questions about which congressmen are
required to make a reasoned judgment is substantial. The homework
necessary to make a sound and independent decision on the subject of
bank holding companies will be of little aid to the congressman when
he is forced to make a recorded decision on other matters. None of
these issues is very much related to bank holding companies or, for
that matter, to each other.

Technical Complexity

Perhaps the number and scope of decisions asked of congressmen
would be manageable if Congress wrote policy in the round. But

Congress, for the most part, does not operate that way. Most legislative proposals are complex, specific, and technical; they order specific actions in specific cases in an attempt to cover many contingencies. They attempt "fine tuning" around an already existing body of legislation that is itself specific and technical.

Congress had twice before passed statutes aiming to separate banking from other commercial enterprises. The first time, partly as a result of the stock market crash of 1929, the Glass-Steagall Act of 1933 focused on the relationships between banks and the sale and distribution of securities. Bank holding companies were not, however, subject to regulation under that law, and Congress saw fit to bring them under regulation in the Bank Holding Company Act of 1956. At that time only multiple-bank holding companies were made subject to federal regulation, apparently because the very few one-bank holding companies in 1956 were small and viewed as innocuous enterprises posing no threat to a competitive economy. By 1969 this was no longer the case. In a rash of mergers, the one-bank holding company had become the vehicle for massive economic concentration. That set the stage for HR6678, a technical adjustment to an existing policy and body of law. There was little debate over basic principles on the House floor, the focus of attention was, instead, on the technical questions of fitting a long standing policy to changed conditions.

Time Limitations

This mode of decision-making requires technical knowledge and time. Time devoted to developing technical competence in one or a few policy areas is subtracted from that available to consider everything else. "Now the years that I studied military things," a member of the Armed Services Committee comments, "it would take a man that many years to learn it. And you just don't have enough hours, enough years, in your life to learn all you should." Time available to members for the evaluation of legislative proposals outside areas of special interest to them is reckoned not in years, but in hours or minutes per week.

We asked our sample of one hundred members how much time each of them spent in legislative study, on the average, outside of the area of his primary interest and activity. The question was difficult (because study time has pronounced seasonal variation) and probably sensitive as well. Even if justified by the special circumstances of congressional life, admission of less than adequate study of the public's business is unflattering for both self and public image. Of 100 members, 58 either did not answer the question at all or gave answers that were too evasive to be codable (Table 2-1). Of those 42 who did give reasonably precise answers, 8 (19%) said that they spent an hour or more per day in such study, 11 (26%) said they spent between 30 minutes and an hour, and the majority, 23 (55%) said that less than 30 minutes per day was devoted to any kind of legislative study outside of their primary areas of interest and activity.[5] A few confess a little sheepishly that they spend *no time at all* in legislative study outside the areas of their special interest and activity.

The real deficiency that's present in the whole scheme of things [one member said] is a time for reflective and unhurried thinking about legislative propositions that are before us. And the schedule around here affords us very little of that time. Most of my time of that sort comes on airplanes flying back and forth to the district. And I think the chief value

TABLE 2-1   AVERAGE DAILY TIME SPENT IN LEGISLATIVE STUDY OUTSIDE OF RESPONDENT'S AREA OF SPECIAL INTEREST AND ACTIVITY, IN MINUTES

	Number and Percent	Percent of Codable Responses
30 or less	23	55
31 to 60	11	26
60 or more	8	19
Noncodable responses	36	—
No answer	22	—
Total	100	100

of an airplane flight to the district is—it gives you time to think. If you're
lucky enough to sit down with strangers on both sides of you, frequently
you may get to spend an hour or two, uninterrupted, to think about
what's going on . . .

Whatever it is that members consider "study" to be—reading newspapers or committee reports, listening to debate, or just thinking—there is consensus among them that they do not devote adequate
time to it. The result is clear; "It takes a comparatively small time
because," says a member, *"we don't do it in depth."*

The standards of members' personal legislative research outside of
their areas of expertise are consistent with the demands imposed by
the number, scope, and complexity of decisions that have to be made.
Although research by congressional experts and their staff is often of
high quality, it is unreasonable to expect that most members will have
the time and other resources necessary for an adequate job. The
congressional definition of what is "adequate study" is thus
considerably different from the naive expectations of many outside the
Congress. One member even speaks of doing study *"in depth"* while
the roll call is proceeding.

A measure of the extent of study by nonexperts is how frequently
they actually *read* bills or, alternatively, committee reports.

Table 2-2 indicates that many roll-call votes are cast by members of
the House without benefit of a reading of the bill or committee report.
When account is taken of the laxity of our definition of "frequently
and regularly," (25% or more of the time) and the number of noncodable (i.e., evasive) answers (11%), this impression is strengthened.

If members had the time to make independent analyses of all legislation, would they have the necessary information at hand? The
answer is yes and no. Information of a sort exists in superabundance
in the congressional environment. Facts and figures on anything and
everything are available in committee reports, from the Congressional
Research Service, from lobbyists, from staff studies, and the mass
media. There may even be too many facts and figures, because the
processing of such information into a Yea or Nay vote is time consum-
ing and, as we have noted, time is very limited. "There's really no

TABLE 2-2 FREQUENCY   OF   READING   COMMITTEE   REPORTS   OR
          BILLS[a]

	Number and Percent
Never	4
Occasionally and intermittently	44
Frequently and regularly	41
No answer, noncodable response	11
Total	100

[a] Specialty and nonspecialty related.

problem," one member says, "in getting the information or in satisfy-
ing your own curiosities as it were, *if you have the time to do it*—the
only element is time." But information of another sort is not so readily
available. Answers to such questions as, "Is this legislation consistent
with my voting record?" or "How will my constituents feel about it?"
or "How will they be affected?" or "What will be the impact of this
legislation?" are not easy to obtain. Thus the congressman who seeks
to undertake independent analysis of legislation risks drowning in a
deep well of facts while at the same time failing to find answers to the
questions about which he is most concerned.

When Davidson, Kovenock, and O'Leary asked a sample of
members of the Eighty-eighth Congress what were "the most pressing
problems you face in trying to do your job as Congressman?" and
"the most pressing problems which prevent Congress from doing what
you think it ought to do?" They found that:

> The most frequently mentioned problems were associated with the com-
> plexity of decision-making: the lack of information, the volume of legisla-
> tion to be considered, and the difficulty of making a rational choice from
> among many conflicting alternatives.[6]

Sixty-two percent of their respondents *volunteered* an answer that
mentioned one or more of these related problems of decision-making,

far more than mentioned such common gripes as the seniority system, the Rules Committee, or pay, office allowances, and staffing.[7]

The Limited Utility of Staff Assistance

Adequate staffing has often been suggested as a cure for these difficulties. The extent to which the cure works appears to be sharply circumscribed. At the time of our interviews members were allowed to have 11 staff members on their congressional payroll, or 12 if the district they represented had a population greater than 500,000. Yet many had no *legislative* assistant at all. "I don't have any staff assistant or research man on my staff," comments one. "I have a staff that is geared to mass production for the district." Such an office setup is not unusual. Other members have legislative assistants, but use them for work in the member's own area of specialization, and receive no personal staff aid outside of their areas of expertise. "The typical member probably does not have real legislative assistance," a member says. "So far as I know most of the staff are technicians of one sort or another. They're not primarily directed at what is immediately coming up. So you're pretty much on your own."

Of the 31 members who reported that they rely on their staff frequently and regularly (see Table 2-3), some also commented that it did not help much; staff members might be good researchers but they were not politicians.

TABLE 2-3   MEMBERS' USE OF STAFF FOR LEGISLATIVE RESEARCH TASKS

	Number and Percent
Never	28
Occasionally and intermittently	36
Frequently and regularly	31
No answer	5
Total	100

We have a staff meeting and at that time my legislative assistant will report on the legislation that is coming up in the week, and will give a brief description of it. In all candor I must say that this does not often influence my thinking on the bill. . . . If it hasn't come up at our [state party delegation] breakfast, I'll run to a guy on the floor just about the time the bill is being considered and say, "Hey, what is this all about and what does it do?" And frequently we'll check with the door-keeper . . . who has a pipeline into the leadership and into those committee members who are responsible for it. I'd much rather be able to answer that my staff thoroughly briefs me on pros and cons in the quiet of my office, and that's how I make up my mind, but that is not true. I think that is really natural. A staff member is reading the cold lifeless reports. They have not been exposed to the various pressure groups or the "gut" arguments for or against something. I think the congressman himself involved in that area, who's been on the firing line, can give you a much better capsule than the more isolated staff man.

The Desire to Be Reasonable

Despite all these difficulties congressmen seek to cast their votes as rationally as possible. All we mean to say here is that when faced with the necessity of casting a Yea or Nay vote, congressmen attempt to cast the vote so as to enhance the chances of achieving their goals. Different congressmen pursue quite different goals—reelection, power and prestige in the House, the approval of the editorial writers of *The New York Times*, a good shot at a seat in the U.S. Senate, the framing of policy in the national interest—but congressmen do have goals and try to use their votes on the floor of the House to enhance the probability of attaining them. A few "bad" votes may not significantly alter the congressman's chances for successful goal attainment, but the innate prudence of ambitious men dictates strenuous efforts to avoid mistakes and to calculate the consequences of their actions and votes as much as possible.

Moreover, previous research on legislative roll-call voting suggests that the voting records of most congressmen display properties that are consistent with rational behavior, or more precisely, are sharply in conflict with what could be expected if congressmen regularly voted in

extremely irrational ways.[8] The members seem to be following relatively predictable decision strategies in casting their Yeas and Nays.
The potential payoffs to congressmen for casting roll-call votes in a
fairly rational way are sufficient, and the potential risks of following
any other course so large, that members try hard to be reasonable.

The context of congressional decision-making thus can be sum-
marized as follows: There are too many decisions to be made across
too wide a span of subjects; the issues involved are too complex for
quick decision, and there is too little time for anything else. Even so,
the congressman must cast his vote in a reasonably rational way or
face the possibility of failing to achieve his personal and political ob-
jectives.

How then, given this perplexing situation, do congressmen make up
their minds?

SOME PARTIAL SOLUTIONS

> . . . it's not uncommon for me to go to the floor with the bells ringing,
> votes being taken, and it's on a bill or issue that I have never heard of
> before [one member said]. I haven't the remotest idea of the issues in-
> volved. You've got to make up your mind. You can't vote "maybe" and
> you can't vote "present"—you don't want to. So you have to make a de-
> cision on the best basis you can.

The context in which ordinary members of the House of
Representatives normally cast roll-call votes does not permit rational-
comprehensive decision-making. The self-conscious setting of goals,
the weighing of costs and benefits of alternative courses of action, and
the choice between alternatives on the basis of goal optimization are
difficult under the best of circumstances. Given the conditions we have
described above, this sort of decision-making can rarely be ap-
proximated on Capital Hill.

The authors of civics textbooks—and their readers—may despair at
this. But students of legislative behavior have long postulated that
other modes of decision are frequently employed by members of
Congress. These other ways of choosing between policy alternatives
are thought to require less time and information than rational-

comprehensive decision-making. We examine some of these modes of decision below in an effort to assess their adequacy as low-cost–low-information substitutes for the unattainable perfection of rational-comprehensive decision-making.

The question we ask about each of these low-information strategies is: Can this be a reasonable description of the *method* members use to make decisions? What variables ultimately *influence* decision outcomes are not in question here; our concern is decision *processes*. We shall see that an influence may be reflected in voting patterns without having been the operative decision process.

Voting the District

One way members of Congress may cope with their problem of decision-overload is to follow the will of their constituencies. Not only does this strategy enhance the congressmen's chances of reelection, but it also relieves them of the difficult task of policy analysis and appraisal. Moreover, a strong argument can be made that this is the strategy of decision members *ought* to follow in a democratic land.

But voting the district is not always easy, because it may be difficult to learn what "the district" wants:

> The longer I'm here the I'm convinced that very few constituents are aware of how I vote. . . . I'm also convinced that a great majority of them have adopted the policy, "We sent you there; now make up your own mind!" That's the reaction I get. On my trips home I always urge them to write. I often get the response, "Well, why should we write and say what we think; that's why we elected you."

Members' information sources about their constituencies are poor. Mail, for instance, is seldom useful to the member in assessing the opinions of constituents:

> I have always thought that the most difficult problem I have in this job was the matter of communications. . . . I would have to say that most of the people in my district do not know what is involved in major legislation. And I would also have to say that not very many of them are

interested. . . . Now there are some exceptions. People generally get pretty exercised over bills concerning . . . things that they can understand readily. The greatest amount of mail we've ever received on any subject was on Daylight Savings Time—unsolicited mail.

"I've seen a lot of interest develop on . . . high-friction issues," says another member, "but on the average legislative calendar we may go three or four weeks without . . . any expression of how any substantial number of people feel." "High-friction issues" are not by any means those most crucial to the survival and prosperity of the Republic, or even necessarily relevant to pending legislation. During the three-month period of our congressional interviews, while the antiballistic missile and tax reform captured newspaper headlines, the hottest subject of legislative mail was the congressional pay raise—months after the fact.

Letter writers are a biased sample of constituencies, and members discount the import of their mail accordingly. Congressmen like to receive mail, not for its information value, but because it gives them an opportunity to communicate in a personal way with constituents. The election-day payoff of the "personal touch" is widely acclaimed on Capitol Hill.

Congressional newsletters and polls are similarly ineffective for information gathering, and similarly effective for other purposes.[9] Communication between member and constituents on *legislative* matters is overwhelmingly in one direction, from member to constituent, and not the reverse. "It is a curious kind of relationship," concludes one member, "because even if you wanted to, you couldn't rely on your constituents to really be the decision-maker for you." As V.O. Key commented in *Public Opinion and American Democracy*, "a legislator . . . is rarely faced by the difficult choice of rejecting or accepting the mandate of his constituency, for he does not know what it is. And, indeed, there may be none."[10]

For most members, and on most issues, the electoral process does not serve as an effective communications medium. Stokes and Miller, reporting on the 1958 elections, found that, "By the most reasonable count, references to current legislative issues comprised not more than a thirtieth part of what constituents had to say about their congressmen."[11] They conclude that, "Although perceptions of individual candidates account for most of the votes cast by partisans against their parties, these perceptions are almost untouched by information about the policy stands of the men contesting the House seat."[12]

Asked how often they thought their constituents either knew or cared how they voted on specific legislation, our 100 members credit constituents with somewhat more issue awareness than does the voting-behavior literature. Still, of those responding, 79 percent said their constituents "seldom" knew or cared how they voted (see Table 2-4). Testing the wind of constituency opinion is not likely in most cases to produce trustworthy cues for behavior.

In the absence of constituent opinions on most legislative issues, it might be assumed that members could anticipate what the opinions would be *if they existed.* Research bearing most directly on this assumption shows only limited support for it.[13] The picture of the local boy in Congress easily anticipating the views of "the folks back home" we find inconsistent with the way members describe their districts:

> My district is terribly miscellaneous, as a lot of districts are. I have a suburban county whose residents [commute], . . . a mixed county [with] onion farming and dairy farming—it is industrial too, . . . an industrial and resort [county], . . . an egg producing county, . . . [and another] is largely dairy farming, although it has some industry too. What are the interests there? The interests are miscellaneous, the interests are general. It would be anything from farm price support to Housing and Urban Development grants for sewers. Are they ideologically conservative or liberal? They run the gamut there too. . . .

Other members see the same complexity, but along different dimensions:

> It is a very diversified district. I have, for example, eight to nine percent Negro. I've got some Spanish and Mexican Americans. I've got pockets of Polish, Italian, Dutch, German from old settlements of 50 to 100 years

old. I've got new suburbia, which is a complete hodgepodge of people. I've got steel. I've got machine tool industry. I've got two auto assembly plants. I've got all sorts of light and small industries—completely diversified industry. So completely diversified industry and completely diversified populations; some real old stable towns, brand new towns where people don't have roots yet. It is so diversified that there isn't any single element, any at all, that I feel stands out.

"Interesting," "diversified," "variety," "cross-section," "heterogeneous," "difficult," these words appear repeatedly when members are asked about their districts (see Appendix A, Question 22). However, many congressmen apparently subscribe to the notion that *other members'* districts are simple and homogeneous, because a typical response to our question was an assertion that the respondent's district was atypically complex.

The pictures members paint of their districts are noteworthy for their scope and detail. Men in the business of being reelected are forced to understand the social fabric of their constituencies. The degree to which the members we interviewed demonstrated such an understanding was impressive, particularly measured against the unflattering images of the congressional mind current in American political culture.

When asked what were "the most powerful groups or interests" in

TABLE 2-4   FREQUENCY WITH WHICH CONSTITUENTS KNOW OR CARE HOW CONGRESSMEN VOTE ON SPECIFIC BILLS

	Number and Percent	Percent of Those Responding
Never	0	0
Seldom (1–25 percent of the votes)	63	79
Frequently (25–75 percent of the votes)	16	20
Almost always (75 percent or more)	1	1
No answer/noncodable	20	—
Total	100	100

TABLE 2-5 PERCEIVED DIMENSIONS OF CONGRESSIONAL DISTRICTS
PERCENT OF RESPONDENTS MENTIONING EACH DIMENSION

Dimensions	Percent Mentioning	
Party	42	(N = 100)
Ideology	29	(N = 100)
Social class	29	(N = 100)
Type of communities	47	(N = 100)
Interest groups	80	(N = 100)
Private nonpolitical groups (e.g., churches, newspapers, universities)	25	(N = 100)

their districts, members responded in terms of a number of familiar dimensions (see Table 2-5). But they viewed these dimensions in a more complex way than the usual urban/rural or labor/management bipolarities employed by journalistic and academic analysts. Members make fine distinctions about the makeup of their constituencies. And where outside observers see simplicity, members, close at hand, see complexity. They typically see their constituencies along more than one relevant dimension. The number of dimensions they use in describing their districts tells us something about the complexity of their perceptions (see Table 2-6).[14]

The commonly accepted notion of congressional district homogeneity is a relic of an earlier day, before massive urbanization, suburbanization, industrial relocation, and reapportionment. Anticipating attitudes is no easy job when a district is complex in social and economic arrangement, attitudinally mixed, and constantly shifting. Nonetheless, congressmen must still do right by the folks back home.

I've found out this much. When you are voting right, you build up points on a cumulative basis. You lose them on a geometric basic; you can lose all your points on one vote. . . .

But "voting right" from the constituency point of view is not much easier than voting on the basis of an independent appraisal of the merits of legislative proposals.

Personal Precedent and Incrementalism

Students of the appropriations process in Congress have noted the influence of past decisions in determining present and future ones. Both the House as a whole and individual members have established precedents on appropriations votes, and such precedents are an obvious simplifying device when new decisions have to be made. "Budgeting is incremental," Wildavsky notes. "The beginning of wisdom about an agency budget is that . . . it is based on last year's budget with special attention given to a narrow range of increases and decreases."[15]

The appropriations process in itself accounts for a substantial proportion of House roll-call votes, but does not exhaust the range of situations where precedent may be an important strategy of decision-making. Some theorists see policy making in general as an incremental operation.[16] Existing policy is altered around the edges, never revised wholesale. It is ratified and modified simultaneously, much like the budget, with its "base" and "increment." There is a core policy and

TABLE 2-6 PERCEIVED COMPLEXITY OF CONGRESSIONAL DISTRICT

Number of "Dimensions" of District Mentioned	Number and Percent	Percent of Those Responding
1	10	11
2	27	31
3	24	28
4	20	23
5 or more	6	7
No answer/noncodable	13	—
Total	100	100

an incremental modification, as in the bank holding company legislation described previously. Such decision-making is an accomodation
with the limits of human perception or, in Herbert Simon's terminology, human computation.[17]

Incrementalism *is* a strategy for reducing the difficulties of decision-
making; but the degree of such reduction must be examined lest we
reach mistaken conclusions about its role in the decision-making
process. Incrementalism, as practiced by the Congress, reduces the difficulty of decision-making, but not sufficiently to make independent individual decisions practicable. To say that a piece of legislation is a
policy increment is not to say that it is easy to evaluate in anything but
a relative sense. Probably only in the appropriations area does the
incremental nature of legislation make for quick and easy decision.
Other factors work to complicate the appropriations bill.[18]

Personal precedent on recurring issues is an obvious simplifying
device. "After you've been around here for a while," a senior Republican says, "why you find that most of these subjects you've had an
exposure to sometime before. They come back again, and so they're
not as strange as they may seem the first year or two." Either for the
sake of consistency or to make an easy decision—or both—the member
can simply vote the same way he did the last time around.

But personal precedent is less valuable as a decision strategy than it
might seem at first glance. It is a truism to say that nothing ever
remains the same, but it is a truism that fits the facts of congressional
life. Even if the legislation to be decided upon is identical to past legislation on which the member has a position, circumstances change.
Public opinion, party positions, parliamentary and strategic considerations—all these can and do change from year to year, making
precedent voting difficult. A bad bill in one session may be the lesser of
evils in another, and compromise that had to be accepted before may
no longer be necessary.

Ideology

Of all the shortcuts to rational decision, the rationale for ideology is
perhaps the most compelling. Ideology is an elegant solution to the

problem of making reasoned choices from limited information on matters of great complexity. It structures choice by invoking uniform criteria to handle disparate issues. Discussions of Congress are frequently cast in ideological terms. "Liberals" vie with "conservatives" for the support of "moderates" to see who will carry the day. Implicit in such discussions is the notion that legislation can be arrayed on an underlying ideological dimension (or dimensions) shared by most members. Ideology then simplifies decision-making because decisions do not have to be made on each legislative proposal *de novo*. Once their ideological implications are known, large sets of bills are responded to in the same way.

The concept of ideology is far from neutral for many members of Congress. But the normative connotations are positive for some and pejorative for others. For some ideology is "principles" and "philosophy of government;" other see it as a kind of mindless knee-jerk reaction. These differing connotations may well explain why we find no consensus about how often ideology is involved in decision-making. We asked how often bills had "sufficient ideological flavor" that voting decisions could be made "largely on the basis of ideology." Table 2-7 shows a considerable spread of estimates of the frequency of ideological voting.

TABLE 2-7 FREQUENCY WITH WHICH IDEOLOGY IS A MAJOR
FACTOR IN VOTING DECISION (PERCENT)

	Democrats (%)	Republicans (%)	All Respondents
Never	6	10	10
Seldom (1–25 percent of votes)	32	44	48
Frequently (25–75 percent)	34	24	37
Almost always (75 percent +)	2	6	5
No answer/noncodable	26	16	—
Total	100	100	100
	(n = 50)	(n = 50)	(N = 79)

The virtue of ideology *as a decision strategy* is economy. Perhaps that explains the resentment of nonideologues:

> I try to approach all problems with an open mind. I think I am neither "pigeonholable" as a conservative or as a liberal or as a dove or as a hawk. And this makes you work a little harder as a matter of fact, because if you don't think about these things too much, it's awfully easy to make up your mind very early in the game as to what your stand is going to be. . . . I am impressed by congressmen who you can't put into boxes. I know that _____ is always going to find out the liberal position and vote that way. And I know_____ is always going to find out what the conservative position is and vote it that way. I like the ones who think about these things and jump around.

Under ideal circumstances, a decision at one time on ideology can dictate a whole series of later decisions, rendering them virtually automatic (pejoratively: knee jerks). In order for ideology to function in this way a number of conditions must be met. One obvious one is that members must, in fact, have ideologies.

An ideology, borrowing from Converse,[19] is a political belief system that has (1) broad scope—including most political phenomena, (2) abstract "objects of centrality," and (3) constraints—exclusions of inconsistent beliefs or elements. It would be possible to measure the degree to which these three criteria are met in the congressional mind in a reasonably precise fashion; we have not done so. But, our largely impressionistic estimate is that about three-fourths of the members of Congress might be characterized as having ideologies by this standard.[20] They are not necessarily ideologues in the sense of being primarily motivated by ideology, but they have reasonably consistent, reasonably abstract, and reasonably inclusive views of politics and government. Others, like most members of the mass public, seem to think only in terms of the concrete, and demonstrate little structure that relates elements of their belief systems to one another.

If members are to use ideology as a decision shortcut, *bills* must have ideological content. If the ideological decision process[21] is to be economical, that content must be *manifest*. Even when only bills subject to roll-call votes are considered it is clear that many have no manifest ideological content.[22] In others, such as the long and complex appropriations bill, ideological issues may be well hidden:

> Well you have to support an appropriation by and large or that agency doesn't run next year. So does that or does that not have an ideological content? Not that much I wouldn't think. But if there's an effort to slash 5 or 10 percent off of it, then that amendment would have an ideological content. My reaction to that would be highly predictable. When it comes to certain selective programs, and there's an effort to slash them, you couldn't always be certain as to how I feel about them. If I made an assessment that if we cut 40 million dollars for peanut research, and I had some feel that that would leave a little more room for food stamps (and that incidentally is a spurious illustration), then I might vote to slash peanut research you see. So I'm not entirely predictable . . . .

Other legislation involves ideological disputes, but in combination with so many technical details that conflicts are obscured:

> Those [bills] with strong ideological flavor oftentimes are very complex, and the ideological flavor may be so distorted by the complexity, or so watered down by the other sorts of things that are present, that you don't get a great clear ideological issue standing all by itself with no concern about what the mechanics are. You may even find in some of these bills that you like the goal for which it is reaching, but the procedure is impractical for one reason or another, and therefore you end up opposing a bill [with] which you agree in principle.

"Ideology is not frequently involved," says another member, "because most measures are amendments to existing laws in which the ideology is already submerged in a lot of legislative detail, and it would be hard to identify." Legislating for a complex society requires "a lot of legislative detail," if it is not to be so abstract and vague that inevitable decisions over details (which may themselves be crucial policy decisions) are passed on to the executive and judicial branches of government. Even the great controversies of the day are clouded by such complexity. "I don't think I would ever decide on ideology in that sense," comments a leader of the House liberals. "If you're thinking of (something like) a bill entitled 'A Bill to Help Poor People,' which I normally would want to help—would I vote for it just on that? The answer is, Hell no, it could be a screwy way of helping poor people."

Respect for legislative craftsmanship runs high in the Congress, even among ideologues. "I think you've got to read the fine print," a liberal says. "What is going to be the practical impact of this? I would put more stress on that. It can sound great, but if it isn't going to work . . . ?"

Ideological voting is probably easier for conservatives. It is easier to make ideological decisions if you are against change than if you are for it—evaluation of the details of implementation is unnecessary if the goal itself is opposed. "I don't have much trouble," one conservative member says. "Maybe that's not very complimentary to me. I don't say it is black and white, but usually it's pretty clear. Well anything that tends to place more control over the individual—I'm just against it!" But conservatives too have their ideological difficulties:

> When you get into, let's say, the Supersonic Transport, I have an interesting time debating that within myself. On the one hand I'd be saying, "Well let's save money and let's be economizing." But I also may be saying to myself, "Why should the Government be underwriting so much of the cost? Why don't the airlines who are going to build one and make the profits do it?" Then on the other hand another part of me is saying, "You can't let the Russians get ahead in this field." So really on that bill I'd have an awful time, . . . because two different philosophical views in that one can't be reconciled.

Issues of legislative strategy also confound ideological simplicity. It is not enough for the member to decide whether he likes or dislikes a bill. If he favors it, is it the strongest bill that can be passed? If strengthening amendments are adopted, will that doom it on final passage? Can liberalization that can't succeed in the House be attained in conference? Should the bill be watered down to insure its success? The wise member who opposes a bill may want to vote for strengthening amendments that will be unpalatable to a majority of the house, ultimately killing the bill. Such difficult problems are commonplace, and their complicating effects on decision-making erode the possibilities for *simplification* of decision-making by ideology.[23]

Finally, if legislation is to be judged ideologically its ideological content must somehow be analyzed. "You can't take the name of a bill and vote on it," one member says, "they all sound good." To do much more is to undertake the kind of legislative analysis that is uncommon and uneconomical, at least outside members' legislative specialties. And digging deeply may only illuminate more complex difficulties:

> You so seldom find any given piece of legislation with which you can agree in its entirety. And there are so many of them that are just borderline in your own ideology, and you get to the point of where you have to weigh what, in your judgment, is bad and what's good, and you eventually get to the point of, "Well, here, all these items are pretty good, but look at these over here. Now are these so good that they are worth the price of these? Or are these so bad that you want to sacrifice the good of these?" And somewhere you have to weigh that evaluation and come up with a judgment.

Where more than one ideological dimension is involved, ideology, *as a means of simplifying decision-making,* begins to break down. If multiple dimensions must be assessed and somehow balanced by complicated and ambiguous priority schemes, then decisions are no longer simplified. This is not to suggest that ideology plays no role in such situations, but only that it may not serve as a simplifying mechanism.

Concluding Remarks

Three strategies of decision have been examined in the second half of this chapter. Each is a shortcut method for personal evaluation of the *content* of legislative decisions. "Voting the district," personal precedent and incrementalism, and ideological decision-making are all capable of reducing the congressman's decisional overload. Upon detailed examination, however, all three prove to have limited application. Each appears—and appears to be useful—on the handful of abnormally visible decisions members record each year. But none seems an adequate strategy for the hundreds of "normal" decisions. All make fewer demands on the congressman's limited time and information than does the rational-comprehensive mode of decision-making, but still demand more of these limited resources than most congressmen are able to invest in most of the votes they must cast. How congressmen resolve this dilemma is the subject of the following chapter.

NOTES

1. *Congressional Record* (Daily Edition), November 5, 1969, p. H10573.

2. This and other unattributed quotations following are from verbatim transcripts of interviews with the 100-member congressional sample.

3. The increase since the latter years of the Eisenhower Adminstration is on the order of 300 to 400 percent, not including the new recorded teller votes.

4. *Congressional Record* (Daily Edition), November 5, 1969, pp. H10533–H10617.

5. John S. Saloma, III, *Congress and the New Politics* (Boston: Little, Brown, 1969), p. 184, reports an average weekly study time of 6.9 hours which, spread over a five-day week, amounts to 83 minutes daily, substantially more than the norm for our respondents. His accounting, based on a questionaire completed by 150 congressmen, includes specialty-related work not associated with the member's assigned committee, which may account for the discrepancy.

6. R. Davidson, D. Kovenock, and M. O'Leary, *Congress in Crisis: Politics and Congressional Reform* (Belmont, Cal.: Wadsworth, 1966), pp. 75–78.

7. *Ibid.*, p. 77.

8. See especially D. R. Brimhall and A. S. Otis, "Consistency of Voting by Our Congressmen," *Journal of Applied Psychology*, Vol. 32 (1948), pp. 1–74; D. MacRae, Jr., *Dimensions of Congressional Voting* (Berkely: University of California Press, 1958); H. D. Price, "Are Southern Democrats Different?" in N. Polsby, R. A. Dentler, and P. A. Smith (eds.), *Politics and Social Life* (Boston: Houghton-Mifflin, 1963), pp. 740–756; A. R. Clausen, "Measurement Identity in the Longitudinal Analysis of Legislative Voting," *American Political Science Review*, Vol. 61 (1967), pp. 1020–1035.

9. The average response rate to congressional polls cited by a number of members is 12 percent. Data so obtained are subject to such severe response biases that it would be naive in the extreme to take them seriously. Given the wide-spread use of scientific polling techniques by politicans in recent years, it is not likely that many are that naive. That the congressional poll is a highly effective electioneering technique seems a better explanation of the common use of this costly device.

10. V. O. Key, Jr., *Public Opinion and American Democracy* (New York: Knopf, 1961), p. 483.

11. Donald E. Stokes and Warren E. Miller, "Party Government and The Saliency of Congress," *Public Opinion Quarterly,* Vol. 26 (1962), p. 543.

12. *Ibid.*, p. 545.

13. Warren E. Miller and Donald E. Stokes, "Consituency Influence in Congress," *American Political Science Review,* Vol. 57 (1963) find correlations of .17 (Social Welfare), .19 (Foreign), and .63 (Civil Rights) between members' perceptions of constituent attitudes and actual constituent attitudes on Guttman-scaled "broad evaluative dimensions."

14. See Question 22, Appendix A. The question was open-ended with no probe, and we were not "looking for" the number of dimensions in it. The number of dimensions mentioned is clearly at least in part a function of the respondent's willingness to talk (near the end of a long interview). Some members responded in ways (e.g. "The People," "Taxpayers") that are probably evasions, but cannot be distinguished from undifferentiated perceptions of the constituency. Hence Table 2-6 probably understates the complexity of perceptions.

15. Aaron Wildavsky, *The Politics of the Budgetary Process* (Boston: Little, Brown, 1964). See also Richard Fenno, Jr., *The Power of the Purse* (Boston: Little, Brown, 1966).

16. David Braybrooke and Charles E. Lindblom, *A Strategy of Decision* (New York: Free Press, 1963).

17. Herbert A. Simon, *Models of Man* (New York: Wiley, 1957), see particularly Chapter 14, "A Behavioral Model of Rational Choice," reprinted from *Quarterly Journal of Economics,* Vol. 69 (1955), pp. 99–118.

18. Wildavsky, *op. cit.*, chapter 1 catalogs a list of such complications.

19. Phillip Converse, "The Nature of Belief Systems in Mass Publics," *Ideology and Discontent,* David Apter, (ed.) (New York: Free Press, 1964). The economy of ideology for decision-making is best outlined in Anthony Downs, *An Economic Theory of Democracy* (New York: Harper and Row, 1957), see particularly Chapter 7.

20. In the Eighty-eighth Congress Richard Bolling estimated that 175 members could be classed as liberals, 185 conservatives. The remaining 75 members were not susceptible to ideological classification. Richard Bolling, *House Out of Order* (New York: Dutton, 1966), p. 50.

21. To avoid later confusion with decision processes that have ideological inputs we should clarify here what we mean by "ideological decision process." The process that we envision is an at least semiconscious perception by the member of (1) an ideological dimension, (2) his position on it, and (3) a range of toleration around his position. Thus, for each vote, the congressman asks himself the simple question: "Does this fall within my range of toleration?" and votes Yea or Nay accordingly. The answer, in this model, is based upon the member's independent analysis of the legislation. For a somewhat different conception see Aage E.

Clausen, *How Congressmen Decide: A Policy Focus* (New York: St. Martin's, 1973) Chapters 1 and 2.

22.   Ideology being somewhat in the eye of the beholder, we can only suggest to the dubious reader that he leaf through the *Congressional Record* or the *Congressional Quarterly Almanac* and satisfy himself that this is the case.

23.   These problems in the strategy of legislative decision-making have effects on the role of ideology in decision-making not unlike the problems Downs, *op. cit.*, pp. 142–163, points out in the context of citizen voting in multiparty systems. In both cases the requirement is an extremely high level of information about probable outcomes, with information costs that more than compensate for the economies provided by an ideological decision rule.

CHAPTER THREE

SPECIALIZATION AND CUE-TAKING

Most congressmen are forced to specialize—to focus their attention on one or a few areas of public policy and to develop some measure of expertise in these fields. "It's like the practice of law," one of them explained, "you can't be a trial man and at the same time an office man." Ninety-seven of the one hundred members of the House of Representatives we interviewed agreed, stating that they specialized in one way or another. Nearly two-thirds of them mentioned only one or two narrowly defined specialties.[1]

SPECIALIZATION AND THE COMMITTEE SYSTEM

The significance of the House's system of standing committees has been recognized at least since Woodrow Wilson's time.[2] The committee system and the strategy of specialization by individual members are related to one another, but they are not the same thing.

Table 3-1 shows the central role of committee assignments in legis-

TABLE 3-1 RELATIONSHIP BETWEEN CONGRESSMEN'S AREAS OF
SPECIALTY AND THEIR COMMITTEE ASSIGNMENTS[a]

Specialties Fall Within Jurisdiction of	Number	Percent
Present committee(s) only	43	49
Present and former committee(s) only	6	7
Present committee(s) and others on which member has never served	37	42
Committee(s) on which member has never served	2	2
Total	88	100

[a] Freshmen excluded.

lative specialization. With freshmen excluded, 86 of the 88 specialists
said that the subject matter of their committees was one of their
specialties. Over half (56%) did not go beyond the bounds of present
and former committee assignments in defining their special legislative
interests. "Members do have to specialize," says one. "Naturally they
specialize in matters that come before their committiees. . . . There is
an old saying that when you come to Congress you know a little about
a lot, but gradually you get to know more and more about a few
things, and at that rate you'll eventually end up knowing nothing
about anything."

If it is clear why most members specialize in their committee work,
why do some choose to go outside their formal committee duties to
stake out an area of expertise and activity? Looking at seniority
(Table 3-2), two explanations emerge.

Members with low seniority frequently have been unable to get
committee assignments in areas of their personal interest, hence they
specialize in their committee work *and* in their chief interests, unable
to bring the two together.

When I first came here I wanted to be on the Judiciary Committee, being
a lawyer, [but] didn't get on the Judiciary Committee. Now I have a few
short years of seniority on the other committees that I've gotten on, and

that pretty well limits the areas in which I have an opportunity to be active. . . . Because of my background as a lawyer and former prosecutor I have been active in the field of crime legislation, even though it's not one of my committee assignments.

Some members have a greater *number* of interests than can be accommodated by their committee positions, and that accounts for noncommittee specialization in both low- and high-seniority groups. Of the high-seniority group 10 of the 14 members who claimed noncommittee specialties also said they had three or more specialties while committee assignments are limited to two. "As far as I'm concerned," one says, "I'm very active in many fields, foreign affairs, domestic affairs, and military spending, and the record will show that I take a voice in these affairs. I have never subscribed to the doctrine that because you're on the Agriculture Committee you ought only to participate in those events affecting agriculture."

TABLE 3-2   RELATIONSHIP   BETWEEN   CONGRESSMEN'S   AREAS   OF
SPECIALTY   AND   THEIR   COMMITTEE   ASSIGNMENTS,   BY
SENIORITY[a]

Specialties Fall Within Jurisdiction of	Low Seniority (2–4 terms) Percent	High Seniority (5 or more terms) Percent	All Members Percent
Present committee(s) only	41	57	49
Present and former committee(s) only	2	11	7
Present committee(s) and others on which member has never served	52	32	42
Committee(s) on which member has never served	5	0	2
Total	100	100	100
	$n = 44$	$n = 44$	$n = 88$

[a] Freshmen excluded.

THE NORMAL PROCESS OF DECISION

The tacit assumption of specialization is that some means exists to handle *normal* decisions, those *outside* of members' specialties. Specialization is a partial solution to the problems of decision-making, but it is not costfree. Lack of information "arises with a considerable degree of frequency and in varying degrees of intensity," one member says. "I think that has to be a factor . . . that we tend to become more and more specialized. We therefore have less and less time to read generally on these matters."

The expertise of the congressional specialist is a product of time, and time spent in specialized activities is time taken away from other functions. The other side of the coin of legislative specialization is a dramatically decreased capability of members to deal with matters outside of their specialties.

> That question goes to the heart of one of the greatest difficulties a member has. If a member really works at his job, then his time is so completely taken up in detail, in attempting to serve his constituents, in attempting to help somebody, to go to meetings with people who are here from your district, to go to all the committee meetings and caucuses—that sort of thing. Time is one of the scarcest items of all and you do not have time unless you take it away from some other worthwhile activity to study legislation.

"I'd say the studying of legislation that is not in your own committee, you spend almost no time at all," says another member, "particularly as you get more active in your own committees. I think it's true that the longer you're here, the more you get to know about a very narrow field and the less you know about the general broad field of legislation." That is particularly true of members of two of the exclusive committee (Appropriations and Ways and Means), whose heavy committee responsibilities virtually preclude members' attempts to inform themselves on pending legislation during much of the session.[3]

Specialization produces a wide differentiation in the information bases members bring to decision-making, both because specialists (in their field) know more than generalists and because specialists outside their field know less. The member facing decisions outside of his area of expertise is up against the fact that the congressional experts, those he agrees with *and* those he disagrees with, know a good deal more about the subject than he. They argue on a higher plane, and they debate assertions of fact he must accept or reject largely on faith, lacking the background and time to do thorough research himself. Such resources as he might expend do not take him far, and he is likely in the end to abandon his evaluation of the issue for an easier evaluation of the expert he chooses to follow. That it is easier to evaluate the judgment of a colleague than to evaluate a complex issue is the basis for the most practical solution to the problems of normal decision-making.

Thus, we hypothesize that *When a member is confronted with the necessity of casting a roll-call vote on a complex issue about which he knows very little, he searches for cues provided by trusted colleagues who—because of their formal position in the legislature or policy specialization—have more information than he does and with whom he would probably agree if he had the time and information to make an independent decision. Cue-givers need not be individuals. When overwhelming majorities of groups that the member respects and trusts—the whole House, the members of his party or state delegation, for example—vote the same way, the member is likely to accept their collective judgment as his own.*

Such a cue-taking strategy of roll-call voting makes it possible for the ordinary congressman both to vote in a reasonably rational fashion and to do so on the basis of exceedingly little information. Outside the area of his own policy specialization, the member need only decide which cue-giver or cue-givers to follow on what sorts of issues. This kind of information can be accumulated fairly rapidly through experience and observation in the House. And the results are likely to be much more nearly rational than trying to do the impossible.

WHY TAKE CUES?

Expected Benefits

Congressmen pursue goals—not the least of them reelection. Thus, an understanding of their decision-making behavior requires a look at the

role their recorded votes play in their expectations of future success or
failure at the polls. A senior Republican remarks:

> Are you going to ask me how often I think a key vote is important to my
> political career? Not very often. I used to make a great point of publiciz-
> ing my voting record, and I still do. And every time I have an election the
> Democratic Study Committee has come up with a list of interpretations
> my opponent can use in which I voted against education—against
> everything. And I got so used to answering that now I'm quite cynical
> about how important national votes are. I don't think people pay much
> attention to them. Newspapers don't report them accurately, and the
> procedures of Congress are such that reporting them accurately is made
> even more difficult.

Most members agree that individual votes ordinarily have very little
impact on electoral success. Running errands, writing congratulatory
letters to newlyweds and high school graduates, sending out newsletters and polls, speechmaking in the district—all these activities have
predictable and positive election day payoffs. Individual votes, on the
other hand, seldom have any impact, positive or negative, and
members know it.

> I think it is rather rare that (constituents) know or care how I vote on
> specific issues. I've been told that surveys indicate that at the time of an
> election campaign only approximately 1 or 2 percent of the constituents
> are aware of how a member voted *on even a single issue.*

The assertion of the unimportance of recorded votes requires qualifications. One is that regardless of his position on a bill, the member
exposes himself politically *if he fails to vote.* An articulate
congressman can usually explain his position on an issue to the satisfaction of most constituents, but the charge of missing an important vote
(and thereby failing to represent his district) is embarrassing and dan-
gerous. Random or irrational voting may be politically safer than missing votes. One member says:

> I want them to know how I vote because I think they ought to know how
> I'm voting and politically it's wise for me to do this. So that next year

when I go up for reelection I can have an image in the mind of the
voters—that here is a man who I remember, he voted this way and he
voted that, and at least I know the man up there was working.

Similar efforts to publicize voting records are common.

If the individual votes are not known, many members think that
constituents do have a fairly accurate composite image of their
congressman. "I think perhaps instead of getting called on one
particular vote," a Republican comments, "you establish a reputation
or maybe an image based on your attitude toward a number of votes,
rather than a person saying you voted for this or that specific bill or
amendment thereof." Such images probably have more to do with district activity—speeches, press releases, campaigning, newsletters—than
with roll-call voting in the House. Even if the development of the
image has little to do with individual roll calls, a vote that is in sharp
contrast to the image might be noted:

> I think (constituents) assume we have voted a particular way. . . . For
> example, in my instance I think they feel . . . that I favor civil rights. And
> I think they just assume I vote this way on every issue, and I don't think
> they really check it. I think they really care, and if they ever got any in-
> dication that I didn't do this, they would probably be very disappointed
> and shocked.

A final qualification, and perhaps the most important, is that from
time to time an issue comes along that strikes a responsive chord with
voters. "I don't think (constituents) follow your vote," a Democrat
says, "except on the key emotional issues. And you have to be very
careful and try to judge which ones will blow up into key issues. Right
now it's the pay raises for congressmen—that's a red hot issue."[4]

The potentially emotional issues sometimes comes well advertised;
prayer in school or flag burning are predictably touchy legislative
topics. But sometimes hot issues arise where members do not expect
them. The mild, and at the time popular, bill banning mail-order sales
of firearms after the assassination of John F. Kennedy later got many
members in hot water with their constituents. "All of my people have
guns," a Midwest Republican says. "This touches them directly. And

they may not have known what was involved in the gun legislation
that was pending, but they had heard or read that someone was going
to take their guns away from them or force them to register them. . . "
Electoral difficulty from a single vote is rare, but it has happened.
However remote the possibility, members are aware of that.

The normal vote then does no good for member's electoral future, and is unlikely to do harm. In a complicated and uncertain
world, members try not to optimize the good consequences of their
votes, but to avoid or minimize the bad.[5] They seek a means to make
economical decisions that avoid the snags or hidden issues that are
potentially troublesome. Their aspiration levels are low.

Economy

With low aspirations and a pressing need to make decisions, members
require an exceedingly economical mode of information gathering,
analysis, and evaluation.[6] Under these conditions it makes no sense for
the average member to invest his scarcest commodity in an attempt to
research legislation for himself when experts have already done the job
and packaged the result.

> In that time that you're developing some expertise, you're also finding
> people on whom you can rely in other areas. . . . There are people in
> whom I have a lot of confidence—I take their word on legislation. I can
> learn as much in 10 or 15 minutes' conference on the floor with another
> member that I can trust as I think I would by spending a lot of hours try-
> ing to do research on a field in which I have no expertise. I don't have
> time to do it anyway.

The "capsule summary" from a trusted member of the committee is
a favored congressional device for low-cost decision-making. It gets
directly to the heart of issues in complicated legislation; something beyond the capabilities of the average member operating on a tight time
budget. ". . . Usually I follow the practice of seeking out a member of
the committee that reported the bill, a member in whom I have confidence," says a Southern Democrat, "and in a little while he can give

me a briefing on it that will reveal information that might take me two or three hours to get if I went out and dug it out myself." If congressional communications are divided into "noise" and "information," bills, committee reports, and hearings are mostly of the former and member briefings on the floor mostly of the latter. "Your inputs are rather unusual," a senior Republican says, "because you are talking to members of the committee who are working on it and are experts." Cue-taking is economical.

Members as Cue-Givers

In a study of communication and decision-making within a House subcommittee, David Kovenock reported that a majority of all "influential decision premises" received by subcommittee members concerning legislative matters beyond the bounds of their subcommittee's jurisdiction came from other members of the House.[7] Kovenock suggests a two-step flow of communications based on legislative specialty:

> Preliminary analysis of the data on the outgoing premises of the six (subcommittee) members suggests that a 'two-step flow' of communications exists in the House. . . . Policy specialists outside the Congressional system 'wholesale' communications to parallel specialists within the legislature; these men in turn 'retail' it to others in the House.[8]

The member of the House has unique qualifications for serving in the role of cue-giver. Colleagues are, first of all, peers, and peer-group identification is always potentially influential in decision-making. "There is a considerable body of evidence," McGuire notes, "that a person is influenced by a persuasive message to the extent that he perceives it as coming from a source similar to himself. Presumably the receiver, to the extent that he perceives the source to be like himself in diverse characteristics, assumes that he also shares common needs and goals.[9]

That congressmen identify with one another has long been noted. "Most professions impose a way of living upon a man," Matthews says, writing about the Senate. "Each group has its own distinct problems, shared experiences, special language, and patterns of work. These create an emotional tie to the group which survives the most vigorous intraprofessional rivalry. . . . Much the same is true of United States Senators. Even bitter political enemies in the Senate had many common experiences and face many similar problems, the 'speak the same language,' they identify with each other."[10]

Members of the House have many things in common, but one tie is particularly strong, the traumatic initiation to the chamber through popular election. This provides a tie that gives them a fairly common orientation toward the political world and separates them from outsiders—even those in government—who have not had similar experiences. Social psychologists have noted that a person's liking for a group and adherence to its norms are enhanced by such a traumatic initiation.[11]

The member of Congress is a professional politician, and thus his evaluations of issues can be presumed by his colleagues to be based on *political* expertise in addition to *policy* expertise, on "savvy" or understanding of "gut issues" as some members put it. The member who is "minimizing regret" in his decision strategy is comforted by the fact that his cue-giver has taken the politics of a situation into consideration. It helps of course if the cue-giver has a constituency similar to that of the cue-taker. But on many matters political considerations are the same across most constituencies, and all that is needed is a good sense of politics. "Many times I've picked up the telephone and called a member in the morning," says a senior Southern Democrat. "I say, 'I see the bill's out of that committee—Judiciary Committee, or Labor Committee, and so forth. I don't know anything—what's it all about? Are there any booby traps in it that I ought to know about, you know? And what's your best thinking about it?' And they can fill you in pretty fast." The House is not closed to information from the outside, but its members want outside information screened through the political judgment of the congressional specialists.

Unlike outside sources, the quality of a member's judgment is easy to evaluate. Even after a short period of service together the cue-taker has seen the judgment of other members put to the test many times; he knows how often they agree with him, and that is his best standard of evaluation. Referring to the judgment of their cue-givers, members repeatedly asserted that, "I know them well enough that I would probably come out at about the same point they do." Evaluating the judgment of collegues is a continuous activity on the Hill; it's as much fun as backyard gossip and far more profitable. When issues are too difficult and numerous for independent evaluation, cues from sources of known performance are likely to carry great weight.

Members, unlike outside cue sources, are usually present at the time of voting decision on the floor, always an advantage, but a particularly vital one when their colleagues come to the floor with a limited notion of the issues involved in a vote. Briefings on the Floor, behind the Rail, and in the Cloakrooms may figure more proximately in many decisions than weeks of committee hearings and hours of debate.

Finally, the member is part of an ongoing social subsystem, one that will continue after the issue of the day is forgotten. The member who wishes to remain in good standing in that subsystem is accountable for his advice. Few issues are important enough to risk practicing deception on colleagues, and the potential cue-taker is secure in that knowledge when he selects another member as his source of evaluation. Outside sources are accountable in varying degrees, but none so much as the member. All these reasons lead members of the House mostly to look to their colleagues as sources of voting cues.

VARIETIES OF CUES

We define a "cue" as *any communication—verbal or non-verbal—intended or unintended—that is employed by the cue-taker as a prescription for his vote.* By definition then, cues are influential, although not necessarily decisive. Cue-taking is a "power" relationship in a limited sense. To paraphrase Dahl, cue-givers have power over cue-takers to the extent that they can get cue-takers to do something they would not otherwise do.[12] But the beginning of misunderstanding of the nature of normal decision-making in Congress, a road often traveled, is to impute power to coercion and initiative to the givers of cues. The base of influence of cue-givers, as we shall see in Chapter 5, is rarely related to the possession of sanctions. Equally important, the initiative in the cue transaction comes from cue-takers, who seek out cue-givers in order to economize decision-making. To the extent that cue-takers are influenced, it is largely because they want to be influenced.

Generations of observers of "pressures" on Congress have been deceived about the nature of congressional decision-making, not because they looked in the wrong place for influence, but because they started by asking the wrong question. They should have asked *not where, but whether* pressures were exerted. In our view, if influence can be said to "flow" from cue-givers to cue-takers, it is not from the "pressure" of the former, but the "vacuum" of the latter.

We have treated voting cues as largely homogeneous entities to this point, and they are homogeneous in their role in our theory of decision-making; they provide evaluations to those who are inadequately informed. But the nature of the cue-givers, the process by which the cue is transmitted, and the nature of the cue itself vary.

Cue-Givers: Initial and Intermediary

Cue-givers are of two general types, initial and intermediary; the former are individuals who, because of personal attributes and positions in the legislative structure, are looked to as a source of information and evaluation on legislative issues. The intermediary cue-givers are groups, or the predominant sentiments within them. They have many of the same attributes as individual cue-givers, but their position in the legislative process is quite different. Except in rare cases, they cannot claim, as a group, to have expertise. Their claim is, rather, to have processed—reacted to—the evaluations of experts in a way that suits the proclivities of the cue-taker. They are secondary in the sense that their "positions" both logically and chronologically follow those of initial cue-givers, but their role in the cue-giving structure is not secondary in importance. When members were asked to whom they turn for cues in low-information situations (see Appendix A, Question

14), over 45 percent of the cue-givers mentioned were groups. That estimate may well err on the low side.

Cue Transmission Processes

There are many different means by which cues are transmitted. In some cases the process is highly formalized:

> We have a group that meets on Mondays whose sole purpose is to discuss the legislation that is coming up during the coming week. This is made up of people on different committees who have different points of view. . . . We . . . go around the circle for a statement and discussion of what is happening in each particular individual's committee. This is very helpful to me.

In other instances it is fast, informal, and often even accidental. "You may follow the lead of someone who immediately precedes you in the alphabet," one Republican says. Another comments:

> As the bells ring and we go over to the House floor to vote, the Republican Party has some employees, as do the Democrats, . . . for instance there's a Republican Doorkeeper and a Republican Sergeant at Arms—sort of a duplicate of the ones on the Democratic side. So as you go into the door of the chamber you say, "Walter, what is this vote?" And they say, "This is a vote, final passage of a bill to increase the Coast Guard facilities," or something like that. And if there is any question about it I say, "Well, how are the Republicans voting on it?" He'll say, "Most everybody's voting Aye on this one," or "This is a No vote." I'll say sometimes, "How did Jerry Ford vote on this one?" And he'll tell me. And so this is—if it's a measure that makes sense and everybody's voting for it–well this is usually then the way I will vote.

Cues: Information and Evaluation

Cues themselves vary, along an information-evaluation dimension. All cues include evaluations; some also include factual information in varying degrees. If a member simply watches how other members are voting, and then follows their lead, the cues are purely evaluative; they tell him nothing more than how he should vote, Yea or Nay. Of course he may infer factual information from the voting pattern (e.g., "If all my liberal friends are voting for this bill, it must be a liberal bill"). Indeed, he would have little reason to accept any cues unless he could infer something of a factual nature from the position of the cue-giver.[13]

It is difficult to pinpoint an extreme case at the other end of this dimension, because it involves drawing the line between pure factual exchanges and cues. "Frequently on the Floor," a Republican says, "I will sit down next to a member of the committee and propound specific questions to him, which are not clear to me either from the debate or committee report. . . . " This does not seem to be a case of cue-taking. Factual questions are asked and factual answers expected in reply. Yet, if these questions are the controversial ones, then asking a committee member (whose position is ordinarily determined long in advance of the debate) may well be asking for a cue *and* the facts to support the resulting position. The line between prescriptions and pure empirical assertions can be fuzzy even under ideal conditions. In the congressional setting it is certainly no less so.

DEVIANT CASES

Our theory of normal congressional decision-making by cue-taking contains variables—information costs, expected benefits, and decision costs—which can be expected to produce "abnormal" decisions when they vary outside their normal bounds. Our argument to this point rests heavily on assertions of the normal levels of these variables—information costs are high, expected electoral benefits are low, and decision costs (analysis and evaluation) are high.

Figure 3-1 is a schematic summary of the postulated relationships in two dimensions. (Information costs and decision costs are assumed to vary together here for ease of exposition.) Abnormal decisions result if either or both of two conditions obtain:

1.   Information and decision costs are unusually low;
2.   Expected benefits are usually high.

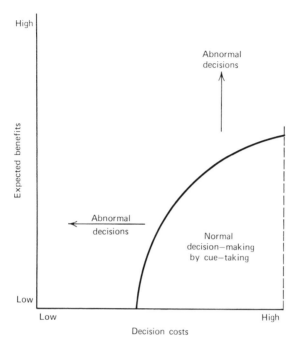

FIGURE 3-1   The range of normal decision-making.

A number of situations occur in which these variables exceed normal bounds.

Types of Roll Calls

Looking first at "deviant" roll calls, we can isolate one situation where all variables tend to exceed normal bounds simultaneously. That is what we shall call the ideological-symbolic vote, typically ringing policy statements that are not expected to have any practical impact. Decision costs are low because of the simplicity of the act—all the member needs to know is whether he agrees or disagrees with the statement. That very simplicity makes these votes more likely to be salient to voters, because they can get a handle on them, and this visibility raises members' aspiration levels. In general then, the more symbolic the act, the more likely members will reach their decisions independently. No other type of roll call is likely to elicit independent decisions from *all* members.

Types of Members

On every roll call some members do not vote by cue-taking. Some, as experts in the field, have already paid the costs of decision and have multiple and complex aspirations associated with the vote. They are likely to be cue-givers.

On some roll calls some members will pay the high costs of decision because the measures are particularly important for their districts. "In that context," a Democrat says, "those particular measures that are of crucial personal importance to your constituency I think are, frankly, very few." But when they do arise, members become heavily involved in the decision process at early stages and continue in an activist role to the last vote.

Finally, those few members of the House who refuse to specialize spread their resources across the scope of legislative activity. They are likely to be somewhat better informed than the average member, but only a little; their resources are still spread too thinly to approximate the level of expertise of the specialists. They are somewhat less inclined to make decisions by taking cues, but only in degree. The line is hard to draw, but some nonspecialists are spread so thinly that they are significantly *more* likely to take cues than other members.

In sum, the theory of normal voting behavior we have developed is bounded by sets of circumstances. We have little to say about those decisions that are beyond the range of our theory, except that they are the decisions to which most of what is said in the literature on Congress is applicable—they are the least difficult to explain in terms of what we already know. In the next chapter we get on with the work of establishing boundaries of normal decision-making.

NOTES

1. The percentages of members answering our question about areas of specialty were: none, do not specialize, 3; one specialty area, 22; two specialty areas, 41; three specialty areas, 19; four specialty areas, 8; five or more specialty areas, 7.

2. Woodrow Wilson, *Congressional Government* (New York: Meridian Books, 1956).

3. The other exclusive committee, Rules, produces generalists because most of the important legislation considered by the House is the subject of Rules Committee study.

4. Congress successfully defused the pay-raise issue by passing the Federal Salary Act of 1967. Under its terms a Presidential recommendation of a pay increase for members of Congress became law unless specifically vetoed by Congress. When the Commission on Executive, Legislative, and Judicial Salaries (and President Johnson) recommeded a $12,5000 pay increase in 1969, the bill to veto it was bottled up in the Rules Committee, evidently to the delight of a majority of the House. Spared the necessity of voting on it, members could get their pay increase and publicly oppose it too. Wayne Hays (Dem., Ohio), speaking of the public opponents of the pay raise in general, and H. R. Gross (Rep., Iowa) in particular said: ". . . he reminds me a little of what Frederick the Great said about Maria Teresa during the partition of Poland—'She weeps, but she takes her share'" *Congressional Record* (daily ed.), March 18, 1969, p. H6666.

5. Minimizing (as opposed to optimizing) models of decision-making have by now a long history in the literature of statistical decision theory. See Simon's "Max-min Rule" in "A Behavioral Model of Rational Choice," *Models of Man* (New York: Wiley, 1957); L. J. Savage, "The Theory of Statistical Decision," *Journal of the American Statistical Association,* Vol. 46 (1951), pp. 55–67; and R. Luce and H. Raiffa, *Games and Decisions* (New York: Wiley, 1957), see particularly Chapter 13, "Individual Decision-Making under Uncertainty."

6. We remind the reader that we are talking about decisions outside the member's primary areas of interest and activity.

7. David Kovenock, "Influence in the U.S. House of Representatives: Some Preliminary Statistical Snapshots," Prepared for delivery at the 1967 Annual Meeting of the American Political Science Association, September 5-9, 1967, see Table 5, p. 25. Kovenock's "influential decision premises" are not quite comparable to our "cues"; he includes purely empirical statements, while we require an evaluative component, but the overlap is substantial enough to make some extrapolation from his data worthwhile for our purposes. Also, since members of his "J Subcommittee" were also involved in the work of the full committee, and some had additional committttee assignments, many of these messages may have been specialty related.

8. *Ibid.,* p. 26.

9. William J. McGuire, "The Nature of Attitudes and Attitude Change," *The Handbook of Social Psychology*, 2nd ed., Vol. III (Reading, Mass.: Addison-Wesley, 1969), p. 187.

10. Donald R. Matthews, *U.S. Senators and Their World* (Chapel Hill: University of North Carolina Press, 1960), p. 68.

11. McGuire, *op. cit., p. 193.*

12. Robert A. Dahl, "The Concept of Power," *Behavioral Science*, Vol. II (1957), pp. 201-215.

13. These inferences may be false sometimes. That explains why some measures with no manifest partisan or ideological content nonetheless elicit roll-call votes with distinct partisan and ideological patterning. For example, our liberal member may follow the cue of a liberal expert, even when the expert's position had nothing to do with his ideology. This "false inference" hypothesis may help to explain the apparent contradiction between member reports of the infrequency of ideological voting and the consistently strong ideological dimensions that emerge from scalogram and factor-analytic studies of roll-call voting.

CHAPTER FOUR

THE INCIDENCE OF CUE-TAKING

INTERVIEWER.   Now we'd like you to try to generalize again, this time about the situation when the member and his staff have not studied the measure and when the interests of the member's constituents are not felt to be particularly involved. How often does this situation occur for the typical member? What about you? When this situation occurs. . . . What do you do?

CONGRESSMAN.   I'd say it probably occurs too frequently. What I'll do on those occasions is . . . , the roll call takes about 30 minutes you know, twice through. I'll then go over to the floor and the members of the committee are sitting at the table for that particular bill. I'll talk to one or two of them. I might talk to Jerry Ford or Les Arends, the two leaders, or the ranking member of the committee, or members of my own delegation. . . . We usually have someone on that particular committee because of the [large] size of our delgation. So I spend. . . . it's not scientific, I'll admit it's not scientific. I'll miss the first roll call, I don't answer the first time through, and that gives me 20 minutes to do a little—it would be a crime to call it research—what-ever-you-want-to-call-it on the floor. . . . [Then] I cast my vote the second time through.

Ninety-five other members of the House—for a total of ninety-six out of our sample of one hundred—responded to this line of questioning in

essentially similar ways. Virtually all congressmen make voting decisions on the basis of cues at least some of the time and under certain
conditions. The aim of this chapter is to describe how often, when,
and under what conditions cue-taking tends to occur.

HOW OFTEN?

Cue-taking is a response to the necessity of choice combined with a lack
of resources—especially time and information—necessary to choose independently between policy alternatives in a reasonably rational way.
Since the shortage of these resources is endemic on Capitol Hill, so is
cue-taking by congressmen. The average member makes voting decisions via cue-taking "frequently," on perhaps one-quarter to three-
quarters of all roll calls (Table 4-1). This estimate was arrived at

TABLE 4-1   FREQUENCY WITH WHICH CONGRESSMEN MAKE ROLL-CALL
VOTING DECISIONS ON BASIS OF CUES[a]

	Number and Percentage
Never	4
Seldom (1–24 percent of roll calls)	17
Frequently (25–74 percent of roll calls)	62
Almost always (75 percent + of roll calls)	4
D.K./N.A./noncodable responses	13
Total	100

[a] Frequency of cue-taking has been estimated from the combined responses
to Questions 10, 11, and 12 (see Appendix A). The numbers in this table
are the frequencies with which those members who take cues in low-
information situations (Questions 11–12) report they face such low-
information voting situations (Question 10). All 13 D.K./N.A./noncodable
responses were from members who say they take cues but were unable or
unwilling to estimate the frequency of low-information situations.

simply by examining the frequency of "low-information situations" for members who say they take cues in such situations. The measure is not precise. It may overestimate cue-taking for some members, because taking cues is not the only response to low-information situations. It probably underestimates the strategy for others, because the stigma attached to admitting that decisions are frequently based on little information is likely to bias interview responses toward underestimates of that frequency. But our purpose here is not so much to estimate the frequency of cue-taking as to illustrate the conditions that enhance or depress it. Our measure serves the latter purpose reasonably well.

Some members, like the one quoted at the beginning of this chapter, feel apologetic about cue-taking. "Congressmen," as another one of them put it, "never talk about it a great deal in public." But most of them learn to live with it:

> You *can't* be knowledgeable about every bill that comes up. But *somebody* knows *something* about the bill. . . . You've got to trust people who know more about a thing because you just don't have enough hours, enough years in your life to learn all you should.

And, for many, the necessary eventually becomes the desirable:

> If I go to the floor to vote in about 5 minutes on a bill that I've never studied, out of a committee that I'm not familiar with, I have on that committee always several personal friends; they're guys whose judgment I trust or general philosophy of government is the same as mine. We vote alike most of the time and I have a very strong feeling that if I had been on that committee and spent the months and years that they have, I know them well enough that I would probably come out about the same point they do. So in these cases that may involve something in which my constituents have no interest, and I'm not familiar, I will say, "What's the wise vote here? Give me a 30-second briefing on the issues" and then go along. . . . You have to make a decision on the best basis you can. The best basis is "What do specialists in the field who have my general philosophy, and whose judgement and savvy I trust, what do they think of it?"

WHEN?

The Nature of the Issue

Voting via cue-taking is more likely to occur on some types of issues than others. It most often takes place when the issue is unusually complex, new, or "nonideological"; when constituents are not actively interested in or informed about the issue; and when the matter is not of major headline importance.

COMPLEX ISSUES.   Almost all issues decided by roll-call votes are more complex than the informed public realizes: but some issues are more complex than others. The sheer volume of technical detail in tax and appropriations' bills, for example, boggles the mind and precludes independent appraisal by most members. Other bills may be less detailed but necessitate more than a layman's understanding of arcane subject matters—nuclear physics, mechanical engineering, agricultural economics, epidemiology, or statistics, for example. The members without training in these fields, or who do not serve on the standing committee reporting the bill, are usually forced to turn to those few members of the House who have some claim to expertise in these areas.

Still other issues are complex because they involve, at least for some members, agonizing choices between cherished values and conflicting policy goals. Witness, for example, the dilemma confronting one articulate spokesman for the poor and champion of "participatory democracy" when confronted with the issue of electoral college reform:

> I'm not sure what I'm going to do with that. I don't know that anybody can help me make up my mind. I just think the notion of popular vote has some defects that haven't been thought through. I fear we've been dazzled by the notion of structuring some mechanical measurement of participation in the Presidential election—that we've ignored the substance of Presidential elections. I think all Americans . . . should be able to vote. . . . And if you count votes then you have to examine what are the ground rules to be able to vote. That leads you to concern about what are the registration laws in the various states and a great deal of the

registration laws severely discriminate against the poor. You can't really believe in . . . just any formula just counts votes. . . . Because the Electoral College at least does count the poor for purposes of translating their votes into results. So I am quite troubled by that one, and I'll wrestle with that one right up to the minute I vote.

He did—and voted for direct popular election of presidents despite his forebodings. No doubt he took comfort in the fact that virtually all other members of the House sharing his ideological persuasion ultimately saw it the same way. And, despite his explicit disclaimer to the contrary, their nearly unanimous resolution of the dilemma in favor of electoral reform *may* have helped him make up his mind.

NEW ISSUES. A substantial portion of the House's legislative business comes up for consideration "over, and over, and over, and over again. You keep getting the same course." Many issues that seem, at first, to pose new problems prove to be "subjects you've had an exposure to sometime before. They come back again, and so they're not as strange as they may seem." "Sometimes you go from English I to English II. . . ."

These recurring and familiar issues do not trigger as much decision-making by cue-taking, at least among more senior members, as the new, the strange, the unfamiliar.

Needless to say, the longer you are here the more you are bound by your voting record. If you've been in favor of international trade and you suddenly start to develop a protectionist attitude towards things, you might find it harder to justify than continuing in the same track. So the longer you are here, the more the pattern of your own votes determines the next one.

But consistency over times is not always possible or desirable. Circumstances change in ways that may compel a reappraisal of long-standing voting patterns. "You get changes when a new administration comes in," the Republican member quoted above continued.

You've been voting to protest against a debt increase. Suddenly with a Republican in the White House—he asks for a debt increase, what do you do? Do you flip-flop, do you try to justify and say, "Now we know in the White House we've a man who's really trying to hold costs down." It's that kind of thing that makes voting interesting. You're never quite sure how you are going to vote yourself.

NONIDEOLOGICAL ISSUES.   Some issues are more readily treated within an ideological framework than others. As we saw in Chapter 2, most congressmen do not feel that many roll-call voting decisions can be made on an ideological basis (Table 2-4), but some of them do. When issues are susceptible to ideological treatment, the more ideological members of the House find the task of decision easier, and cue-taking becomes less essential as a decision-making tool. A Southern Republican provides a good example:

> I tell you basically I've found out a voting record follows certain patterns. . . . One of 'em, for example: usually I favor where it means decentralization. In other words it gives more power to the states than to the Federal Government. So many of the bills are [on] the other side of the fence: they give more power to the Federal Government than they do to the states. So you have a position. Second, there are many bills around here to create more and more bureaucracy in Washington. . . . I'm against bureaucracy. I'd rather combine it, or find a way to combine it. Third . . . is what's your concept of finance? Do you take an attitude that we can just print money over at the Mint and it doesn's matter? Or do you believe that we should have a sound financial system and pay our bills as we go? Well I'm in the sound financial basis of economics [group]. And that will govern you on about half the bills. . . . So you boil it down to these general categories—take foreign aid, that's another category. . . . Now they bring up various bills like the one they brought up this year—$450 million to go through an international development bank. But it wasn't anything but a giveaway. We don't have to research that thing. Really, within 15 minutes it's so obvious what they are doing—you know it's a 50-year loan, no repayments for 10 years—you familiar with that sir? . . .

But the task of decision is not as simple as this member would lead us to believe—even for ideological members on ideological votes. Ideologically inclined members take cues as often as those members who do not feel that ideology is very helpful in deciding issues (Table 4-2). Apparently, the quickest and easiest way to determine the ideological content of bills is to find out the voting intentions of fellow ideologues.

ISSUES ABOUT WHICH CONSTITUENTS DO NOT KNOW OR CARE. When congressmen know how their constituents want them to vote they are likely to go along. But most of the time constituents remain mute, and the member doesn't know what they want, or is reduced to guessing what they would want if they knew or cared about about the issue. As one congressman said, "I feel . . . in a vacuum, because we're physically in Washington much of the year and don't get a chance to get back home and discuss with the people and listen to the people." Unless the member takes his problems directly and personally to his constituents, he doesn't get much policy guidance from them. A silent consituency encourages cue-taking behavior on Capitol Hill.

Constituents, according to members, are more likely to take an active, informed, and articulate interest on some types of issues than on others (Table 4-3). Issues that directly and personally affect

TABLE 4-2 FREQUENCY OF CUE-TAKING BY IDEOLOGICAL AND NONIDEOLOGICAL HOUSE MEMBERS

How Often Member Takes Cues	How Often Ideology Determines Roll-Call Vote	
	Never/Seldom (percent)	Frequently/Always (percent)
Never/seldom	21	19
Frequently/always	79	81
Totals	100	100
	(38)	(32)

constituents are viewed as the most common of these:

> I don't think a majority of my constituents are too concerned about most legislation I vote on because it doesn't affect them directly. When it comes to a tobacco support bill or a farm program of some kind, I think they are very much concerned. But when it comes to providing a flood control project in some other part of the country, I think they have an [economic] interest in it, but I don't think the voter is concerned. When it comes to flood control projects in their area, then they have an interest. Then, of course, their interests are divergent depending upon who owns the land, whose land is going to be flooded, whether or not they are going to get power from it, and things of that kind.

But constituency concern about the voting of their congressman is not solely the result of economic calculation:

> My feelings about consituents is they're very spotty in their interests. They'll get sort of emotionally aroused about a conservation issue, or they'll get worried about Vietnam, or they'll start reading a lot about ABM, and they'll suddenly send a lot of mail—or the gun (control) legislation—they are very spotty. Things that might be of equal importance won't seem to hit any consituent strongly enough to write.

LOW VISIBILITY AND "MINOR" ISSUES. Finally issues on which cue-based voting decisions are common concern low visibility proposals of

TABLE 4-3   TYPES OF ISSUES AND CIRCUMSTANCES WHEN CONSTI-
TUENTS MAY "KNOW AND CARE"

	Percent Mentioning	
Issues of direct personal concern	32	$(N = 100)$
Issues covered by local press and TV	21	$(N = 100)$
"Emotional" issues (gun control, congressional salaries, etc.)	17	$(N = 100)$
Controversial bills of national importance	13	$(N = 100)$
Around election time and during campaigns	10	$(N = 100)$

relatively minor import. The Congress takes up many hundreds of legislative proposals each year. Only a relative handful are viewed as nationally important and receive substantial attention from the news media.

The congressman's information problem is not severe on headline issues. For one thing, extensive newspaper, magazine and television-radio coverage of issues stimulates constituency interest and activity—the congressman is likely to hear something from "the folks back home." Congressmen read newspapers and watch television, too—many of them avidly, complusively. "Most of the reading I've done for all my adult life has been pointed to public affairs. . . ." one such congressman explained.

> By reading *The New York Times* more particularly, but also the [Washington] *Post*, and then your weekly journals of opinion, you can smell whether or not there's something wrong. . . . I rely a good deal on the press, the *Wall Street Journal,* and the *Times*, and I'd say the *Post* do very well in the area. Also if you talk politics during the course of the day you can just hear from your colleagues which issues are being discussed and debated. So you have a feeling what to look for. . . .

On big issues, on issues that are "news," the typical low-information setting for congressional decisions is significantly altered. The members may not be as well informed as we might like, but on major, high-visibility issues they have, as one of them put it, "a general floating knowledge of what it's about" as they head for the floor of the House to cast their vote. Independent appraisal and decision-making is at least possible.

The Parliamentary Setting

The nature of the issue is not the only factor affecting the incidence of cue-taking in the House of Representatives. A number of aspects of the parliamentary setting affect the amount of cue-taking in the process of arriving at a decision in the House.

TIME OF DECISION. As a general rule, decisions made early in the legislative process are more likely to be the result of independent appraisal than those made toward the end. Just as in election campaigns, the interested, informed, and committed tend to make up their minds early in the game; the disinterested and "cross-pressured" tend to make up their minds at the last moment.[1]

Most of the early deciders in the House are policy specialists who serve on the committees and subcommittees that must approve the bill before it comes to the floor. But even those specialists who are not thereby *forced* into an early decision tend, if they are particularly interested and concerned about a legislative proposal, to develop a position early in the lengthy process of House decision (Table 4-4).

The nonspecialists, on the other hand, are not paying much attention to "HR123" because they are interested in "HR456." Nor is there much point for the nonspecialist to give much consideration to proposals outside the areas of his special concern until the matter reaches the floor (save, perhaps, on major headline issues and on matters of such interest to his constituents that he must adopt a position in order to answer his mail). Confronted with a chronic decision-overload, members do not decide issues unless they have to; most legislative proposals never reach the floor. Why try to resolve complex issues that may never come to a vote?

Cue-taking can and does occur at any or all stages of the legislative process. But it is most prevalent at the floor stage.

AMENDMENTS AND UNEXPECTED MOTIONS. Most of the time the members of the House are forewarned that they will have to cast a recorded vote on an issue. Both parties circulate whip notices on Fridays announcing the legislative schedule for the following week, and party leaders usually strive as well to advise their colleagues of changes in the schedule. But sometimes roll calls are held without advance warning. "It's the ones where you don't expect a roll call at all," one member remarked while discussing the problem of low-information voting. "It's that kind of vote that you are *really* ignorant

TABLE 4-4 TIME OF DECISION BY CONGRESSMEN IN AND OUTSIDE
AREAS OF LEGISLATIVE SPECIALIZATION[a]

Time of Decision	In Areas of Legislative Specialization (percent)		Outside of Areas of Legislative Specialization (percent)	
	Earliest Time Mentioned	Latest Time Mentioned	Earliest Time Mentioned	Latest Time Mentioned
Before coming to Congress	18	—	—	—
Before bill introduced	29	2	—	—
At about time bill introduced	18	—	2	—
During hearings	24	14	—	—
During committee deliberations	7	52	7	—
During floor debate	4	10	87	6
Just before voting	—	8	4	24
During voting on floor	—	14	—	70
Total	100	100	100	100
	(79)	(63)	(46)	(50)

[a] Freshman omitted.

about." The member has little recourse but cue-taking in these circumstances.

Voting on amendments also occasions much cue-taking behavior. "Frequently there are amendments that you know are going to be offered, and if the amendment is adopted you can support [the bill], and if the amendment isn't adopted you can't support it. Sometimes you can't anticipate the amendments." In the midst of such parliamentary thrusts and parries even the most expert members can and do become confused and uncertain about the consequences of voting "aye" or "nay." The ordinary member, dashing into the chamber in the midst of a vote on an unexpected and unknown amendment has no more rational strategy than to find what "the good guys" are doing. "That time it takes to call a roll call, that is not wasted time; that's *study* time!"

NONRECORDED AND NONVISIBLE DECISIONS. All other things being equal, cue-taking is more likely to occur on nonrecorded decisions made in private than on recorded, public votes.

But all other things are rarely equal. Most nonpublic decisions are made relatively early in the legislative process by committee members and policy specialists who tend to be relatively well informed. And most nonrecorded floor votes are taken in Committee of the Whole, whose sessions on a bill are disproportionately attended by the members who are especially interested and informed on the issue. Among the less interested and involved nonspecialists, however, the less visible the decision, the more likely they are to make their choice as cheaply as possible—by taking cues.

THE END OF SESSION. Cue-taking is most prevalent at the floor stage. During the early months of each session, relatively few floor decisions are made. But as the committees complete their deliberations and the end of the session draws nigh, action on the floor picks up in a mad dash for adjournment. In the closing days of the session, the pace is so hectic that, for the nonspecialist, independent study and appraisal is out of the question and cue-taking becomes the only course to follow. Unless, that is, the member adopts the decision rule of one Southern Democrat who admits that during the end-of-session crunch he votes "no" on any proposal for change save the motion to adjourn.

WHO TAKES CUES MOST OFTEN?

More than the nature of the issues and the parliamentary situation determine the incidence of cue-taking. Some members have a propensity to take cues; a few struggle to get along without them altogether; most

TABLE 4-5 NUMBER OF SPECIALTY AREAS AND FREQUENCY OF ROLL-CALL VOTING DECISIONS ON THE BASIS OF CUES OUTSIDE MEMBERS' AREAS OF SPECIALTY

Frequency of Voting Via Cue-Taking	Number of Specialty Areas (percent)			
	1	2	3	4+
Seldom/never	10	26	38	0
Frequently/always	90	74	62	100
Totals	100	100	100	100
	(20)	(34)	(16)	(12)

members fall somewhere in between. What factors predispose members to rely heavily upon cues as an aid to decision-making?

First of all, members with relatively narrow, committee-based specialties tend to rely more on cue-taking outside their area of concern than do those with broader legislative interests (Tables 4-5 and 4-6). The Appropriations Committee members are classic examples of specialists who have little time to concern themselves with anything else—all nine members of this committee in our sample indi-

TABLE 4-6 COMMITTEE ASSIGNMENTS, AREAS OF SPECIALTY, AND FREQUENCY OF ROLL-CALL VOTING DECISIONS ON THE BASIS OF CUES OUTSIDE MEMBERS' AREAS OF SPECIALTY

Frequency of Voting By Cue-Taking	Member Specializes in Area of Committee Work Only (percent)	Member Specializes in Committee Work Plus Other Subjects (percent)
Seldom/never	15	36
Frequently/always	85	64
Totals	100	100
	(41)	(36)

cated that they "frequently" or "almost always" voted on the basis of cues. One member explained why:

> . . . a person who's not on the Appropriations Committee or the Ways and Means Committee has a tremendous amount more time to digest the bills that come on the floor. First of all, the Appropriations Committee is the only committee that sits all day long, whereas the other committees if they are going to sit in the afternoon have to get unanimous consent. So they have plenty of time. There is no rhyme or reason why they shouldn't be well prepared on every bill that comes on the floor of the House. Usually, as you know, on Appropriations we're sitting up here while the House is debating. The bells ring and there is a roll call, we're running down to vote. . . .

Members with the very widest range of specialty areas also tend to be frequent cue-takers (Table 4-5). Apparently these men are spread so thin that they, too, have little time or energy left to attempt independent decision-making on the bulk of legislative matters which come to the floor.

Seniority has contradictory effects on the frequency of cue-taking. On the one hand, years of service in the House result in a public record that is usually inexpedient to alter. The more experienced members find it easier to make up their minds on a bill today, because they are publicly recorded as having made up their minds on a similar bill last year. Seniority, therefore, should be negatively correlated with cue-taking, at least on recurring issues. On the other hand, years of seniority tend to result in increasingly burdensome committee and subcommittee responsibilities. Seniority thus tends to encourage a narrowing of the member's scope of legislative concern (Table 4-7). This should have the effect of making senior men more dependent on cues than are their less specialized and less overworked junior colleagues. The net effect of these two self-canceling processes is not great but, on balance, senior members of the House are somewhat more likely than junior men to make voting decisions by means of cue-taking (Table 4-8).

The informal and unofficial group life of the House also affects who takes cues and how often. Entering freshmen of each party regularly

TABLE 4-7 SENIORITY AND NUMBER OF SPECIALTY AREAS

Number of Specialty Areas	Number of Term in Which Member Serving (percent)		
	1–2	3–7	8+
1 or 2	46	55	67
3 or 4+	54	45	33
Totals	100	100	100
	(24)	(49)	(24)

band together into "class" clubs (Eighty-eighty Club, the Eighty-ninth Club, etc., signifying the Congress to which they were first elected) in order to enjoy good fellowship and to exchange information, ideas, and experiences.[2] Most of these dwindle after a few years of activity but, on the Republican side, some have evolved into continuing, broad-based organizations such as the Chowder and Marching Society, SOS, Acorns, and the Wednesday Group. The Democrats are less inclined to initiate and sustain these informal sociolegislative groups than the Republicans, perhaps because of the existence of the Democratic Study Group, to which most Northern Democrats belong.

TABLE 4-8 SENIORITY AND FREQUENCY OF MEMBERS' ROLL-CALL VOTING DECISIONS ON THE BASIS OF CUES

Frequency of Voting By Cue-Taking	Number of Term in Which Member Serving (percent)		
	1–2	3–7	8+
Seldom/never	32	20	19
Frequently/always	68	80	81
Totals	100	100	100
	(19)	(45)	(21)

The Republican groups tend to be small, the number of members approximating the number of standing committees with one member from each committee. These groups meet frequently, normally once a week, and a significant portion of each meeting is devoted to "going around the table," each member briefing the others on issues and political developments within his area of policy speciality. No efforts ordinarily are made to arrive at a collective judgment—which would be difficult, given the heterogeneity of the membership for most such groups—but most members find them a pleasant means of developing friendships and contacts, and a good way of keeping track of what is going on outside their own span of attention.

The Democratic Study Group exists to organize liberal Democrats for effective legislative action.[3] Unlike the unofficial Republican groups, it has its own whip system for ensuring member turnout for critical votes. While it does attempt to inform its members through task force studies and staff reports, its large size prevents the kind of intimate roundtable discussions that are stock-in-trade of the Republican groups.

Members of Republican sociolegislative groups are a good deal less likely to make voting decisions on the basis of cues than are their unaffiliated Republican colleagues (Table 4-9). Democratic Study Group members are as likely be be cue-takers as the other Democrats. All Democrats and unaffiliated Republicans are therefore more likely to be frequent cue-takers than are Republican members of unofficial sociolegislative groups.

Some state party delegations perform an information dissemination role similar to that of the sociolegislative groups. "Our California delegation has communicated very closely," comments a Democrat. "We have one or two members on every committee, and we caucus weekly. And a part of that time is used to exchange views among ourselves. For instance . . . , matters before Interstate and Foreign Commerce, I would tend to know very little about in detail, but would rely very heavily on John Moss and Lionel Van Deerlin." Such a systematic information exchange obviously is limited by the size of delegation and the frequency and regularity of communication. To be

TABLE 4-9 FREQUENCY OF CONGRESSMEN'S ROLL-CALL VOTING
DECISIONS ON BASIS OF CUES BY SOCIOLEGISLATIVE
GROUPS AND PARTY (PERCENT)

	Democrats		Republicans	
	Belongs to DSG	Others	Belongs to Rep. Group	Others
Seldom/never	15	22	40	20
Frequently/always	85	78	60	80
Totals	100	100	100	100
	(27)	(18)	(15)	(25)

fully effective in this role the delegation must be large enough to have members on most of the committees in the House. But similar exchanges may take place in small delegations on a limited basis. In a small delegation members may exchange information on the activities of three or four committees, and look to other sources for the rest.

Regardless of size, frequent interaction is necessary for an ongoing information exchange. Our respondents were asked to rate the interaction of their state party delegation relative to other delegations with which they were familiar. Of those who said that the level of interaction of their delegation was greater than average, 31 percent said that they seldom voted on the basis of cues, while the corresponding figure for those with average or less than average interaction was 13 per cent (Table 4-10). The differences are modest, but it is clear that the state party delegation can function in a manner that significantly raises the information level of its members.

Members of Congress sometimes have to explain their decisions to constituents, and those who do find it necessary to invest more individual study in matters outside of their specialty. "Because I make quite a point of reading most of my mail and I have some fairly articulate constituents who like to write letters, I [have to] do quite a lot of

TABLE 4-10   FREQUENCY OF CONGRESSMEN'S ROLL-CALL VOTING DECISIONS ON BASIS OF CUES, BY AMOUNT OF INTERACTION BY STATE DELEGATION (PERCENT)

	Frequency of Delegation Interaction	
	More than Average	Average or Less
Seldom/never	31	13
Frequently/always	69	87
Total	100	100
	(29)	(38)

studying," comments a beleaguered Republican. Of those members in our sample who report frequent constituent interest in legislation, a somewhat greater proportion, 40 percent as opposed to about 16 percent for those who report little constituent interest, say that they rarely vote on the basis of cues (Table 4-11).

TABLE 4-11   FREQUENCY OF CONGRESSMEN'S ROLL-CALL VOTING DECISIONS ON BASIS OF CUES, BY FREQUENCY OF CONSTITUENCY INTEREST (PERCENT)

	Frequency of Constituency Interest	
	Never/Seldom	Frequently/Always
Seldom/never	16	40
Frequently/always	84	60
Totals	100	100
	(56)	(15)

SUMMARY

The theory of roll-call voting developed in Chapters 2 and 3 led us to believe that the normal vote by the ordinary member of the House of Representatives would be cast on the basis of cues. In this chapter we have tested this hypothesis against what members of the House say about their decision strategies.

While the real world is always more complex than theory, we found substantial agreement between the two in this case. Virtually all members told us that they made up their minds on the basis of cues some of the time; most of them admitted to relying on cues regularly under certain circumstances. The frequency of cue-taking depends on the nature of the issue and the parliamentary situation, both of which can and do affect the adequacy of information the member has when he is forced to decide. And some members are more prone to rely on cues than others. This chapter has been devoted to exploring these relationships in detail.

NOTES

1. For examinations of the effects of cross pressures in delaying citizen voting decisions, see P. Lazarsfeld, B. Berelson, and H. Gaudet, *The People's Choice* (New York: Columbia University Press, 1944), pp. 60-61; and A. Campbell, P. Converse, W. Miller, and D. Stokes, *The American Voter* (New York: Wiley, 1960), pp. 80-83.
2. See C. L. Clapp, *The Congressman: His Work as He Sees It* (Washington, D.C.: The Brookings Institution, 1963), pp. 36-45.
3. See *Congressional Quarterly Weekly Report*, October 10, 1969, pp. 1940-1945; and A. Stevens, Jr., A. Miller, and T. Mann, "Mobilization of Liberal Strength in the House, 1955-1970: The Democratic Study Group," *American Political Science Review*, Vol. 68 (1974), pp. 667-681.

CHAPTER FIVE

THE DIFFUSION OF CUES

Like a vast picture thronged with figures of equal prominence and crowded with elaborate and obtrusive details, Congress is hard to see satisfactorily and appreciatively at a single view and from a single standpoint. Its complicated forces and diversified structure confuse the vision, and conceal the system which underlies its composition. It is too complex to be understood without an effort, without a careful and systematic process of analysis. Consequently very few people do understand it, and its doors are practically shut against the comprehension of the public at large.

Woodrow Wilson, *Congressional Government*, 1885

Compared to Woodrow Wilson's often quoted description of Congress, the picture of the House of Representatives we have presented so far is starkly simple. It consists of two discrete sets of actors—cue-givers and cue-takers. Cue-givers obtain information from outside the institution, process it into a policy decision, and then disseminate their conclusions to the remainder of the membership. The role of cue-giver is not wholly a matter of personal choice; cue-takers decide whose persuasion, speeches, or votes are dependable bases of evaluation to accept as their own. Perceived expertise is the primary basis of this choice.

Wilson's crowded and confused picture, when viewed through the prism of our theory, can be represented by Figure 5-1. This model is intended to describe the last antecedent act to the casting of a Yea or Nay note. This, we think, it adequately does.

But this model of the final decision process raises questions that it cannot answer itself. How, for example, do *cue-givers* make up their minds? And how do cue-takers decide, when the members they perceive to be well-informed experts *disagree*? A more complex model is required before we can address questions of this sort.

TIME, INFLUENCE BASES, AND DIFFUSION

Up to this point we have ignored the time sequence of cue-giving and cue-taking except in noting that cue-givers necessarily must make up their minds before cue-takers. In fact, members of the House do not make up their minds at one or two points in time, but at various moments, sometimes stretching over weeks or months of controversy (see Questions 4 and 13, Appendix A). This fact has important theoretical

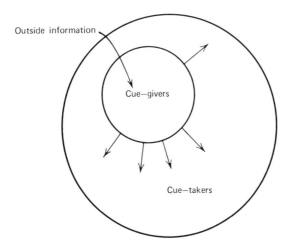

FIGURE 5-1   A two-step model of cue diffusion.

consequences; it permits the same actor to serve as a cue-taker at one point in time and as a cue-giver at a later point. The sharp distinction between cue-givers and cue-takers is blurred by the existence of intermediaries who are both.

Sometimes these intermediaries are individuals but, more often, they are groups. The member faced with the necessity of making a low-information decision is very likely to find out what the "good guys" (by his definition) are doing. If almost all of them are on the same side of an issue, why not take their collective judgment as his own?

But such cue-giving groups are not likely, in most cases, to consist wholly of experts so interested in and informed on the issue that they have made independent assessments of its merits. A Southern Democrat, for example, may be swayed by the positions of his party colleagues from below the Mason-Dixon Line. If so, his choice of cue-givers probably was not dictated by a presumption of expertise on their part, but by other considerations. Or suppose that a Republican decides to make up his mind on the basis of the opinions of House experts. He contacts those members he considers to be especially well-informed on an issue and discovers that they sharply disagree. How then does he choose between them? A theory that argues that cue-taking is the normal mode of decision-making in the House must be able to explain what members do when these experts are in conflict, for experts frequently disagree. It is thus necessary to modify our initial theory to allow for cues based on something in addition to expertise. Following the French-Raven classification on the bases of influence,[1] we view cues as resting on one or more of five bases:

1. *Expertise*—the cue-taker believes the cue-giver(s) is (are) better informed than he either is, or can become without a prohibitive investment of his limited resources.

2. *Reward*—the cue-taker believes that the cue-giver is able to provide tangible assistance in the achievement of his goals.

3. *Coercion*—the cue-taker believes that the cue-giver is able to force him, against his will, to do something he would not otherwise do.

4. *Legitimacy*—the cue-taker believes that the cue-giver has a right to offer evaluations and to have them heeded in the absence of contrary inclinations.

5. *Reference*—the cue-taker identifies with the cue-giver.

The existence of one or more of these influence bases is necessary for a cue transaction to occur, but it is clearly not sufficient. Nor are these bases exclusive; combinations of them are common and more potent than any one of them alone.

The addition of a time dimension, of intermediate cue-givers, and of multiple bases of influence would seem to complicate hopelessly our initially simple picture of the decision-process in the House. The number of possible paths a policy evaluation might follow from its source to the last cue-taker is nearly infinite. But, fortunately, the House of Representatives is not a collection of 435 persons who interact in a random fashion like molecules of gas in a container; the kind of diffusion model that would be appropriate for molecules will not do for the House. Members of the House are structurally defined—by party, state, region, seniority, specialization, membership in informal groups, attitudes towards one another, and so on. Structural regularities of the institution define and limit the way in which information and evaluation are diffused.

A simple model of the decision process in the House of Representatives that accommodates these new elements in our theory might look like Figure 5-2.

A small set of members, especially interested in and informed on an issue, process information from outside the institution into a policy decision. More members adopt the decision as their own on the basis of cues from the initial cue-givers. The undecided members of the House now have two sources of cues to choose from, the *initial* cue-givers and the *intermediaries* who, having made their decisions, serve as alternative cue-givers. While both sets of cue-givers may or may not be emitting the same signals, the situation has been altered by the introduction of additional *bases* for the acceptance of cues. The primary, although not necessarily exclusive, reason for following the initial cue-

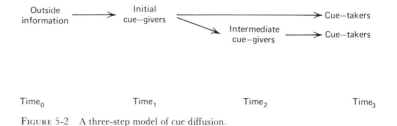

FIGURE 5-2   A three-step model of cue diffusion.

givers is their expertise, real or alleged. They have studied the matter; they know more about it than anyone else. The claim to expertise of the intermediate cue-givers is much less impressive. But as a larger and usually more representative group, the intermediate cue-givers usually possess more *legitimacy* and *reference* bases in the eyes of cue-takers and, less frequently, ability to *reward* or *coerce* undecided members. As the policy evaluation diffuses outward from the initial decision-makers it picks up more and more reasons for undecided members to adopt it as their own.

Of course, the diffusion of voting cues to the entire House of Representatives can and frequently does require more than three steps. When it does, the same pattern applies (see Figure 5-3).

A subcommittee, for example, may make the initial policy decision and its members may serve as the initial cue-givers on a legislative controversy. The parent committee then arrives at a position, in part from subcommittee cues. If the proposal is reported to the floor, influential members of the Democratic Study Group and the "Conservative Coalition" may take positions, largely on the basis of signals picked up from sympathetic committee members. Finally, the formal leaders of the Democratic and Republican parties may become active for or against the measure. All these different individuals and groups, by adopting the decisions of subcommittee members as their own, become available as sources of cues for the yet undecided members. As the group of undecided congressmen shrinks, the number and variety of potential cue-givers and the bases upon which they can choose between them expand. Expertise, the primary reason for accepting cues early in the

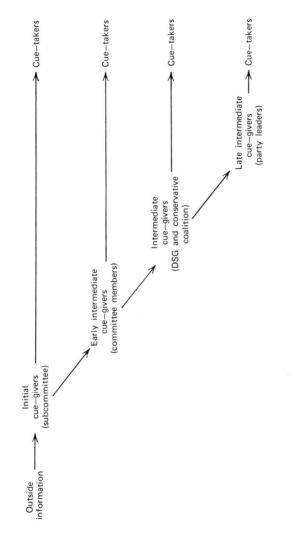

FIGURE 5-3 A multistage model of cue diffusion.

83

process, becomes less important later. Finally the diffusion process ends; the members cast their yeas and nays. The decision of a handful of members has been processed into an authoritative decision of the House of Representatives.

But all this is hypothetical and abstract. Let us see what the members of the House *say* about the diffusion of cues.

THE ATTRIBUTES OF INITIAL CUE-GIVERS

Initial cue-givers are individuals with some claim to expert knowledge. At the very least they are sufficiently interested in a matter to make up their minds early. But as all "experts" are wont to do, they often disagree. How ordinary members, too hurried and preoccupied by other matters to make an independent judgment, choose between competing experts in thus critically important. Some clues to the criteria they employ are provided by member descriptions of those to whom they turn for policy guidance when the time and information at their disposal are exceedingly limited.

Friendship

> Your personal chats with your colleagues who are on that committee I think are very important. In other words, if you have a friend on that committee, who you respect as a man of integrity, seriousness, and intellectual honesty—you ask him and he's almost honor bound to give you a straight analysis of it. I find I rely quite a bit on people I know and think a lot of on [the] committee that has a bill up for debate.

Thus one member describes the impact of friendship in determining which experts will be sought out for advice. Friendship was mentioned as a cue-giver attribute by 31 percent of the sample. It accounted for about one-sixth of all attributes mentioned (see Table 5-1).

The habitual glad-handling and backslapping on the House floor are graphic evidence of members' realization of the value of

TABLE 5-1   ATTRIBUTES   OF   INITIAL   CUE-GIVERS,   BY   PARTY
(PERCENT OF ATTRIBUTE MENTIONS)[a]

	Attributes				
Party	Friendship	Trust-worthiness	Similar Views	Reciprocity	Total
Democrats	17	38	37	8	100 ($n = 98$)
Republicans	16	41	35	7	99 ($n = 85$)
All members	17	39	36	8	100 ($N = 183$)

[a] The number of attribute mentions exceeds the number of respondents because members were free to mention as many or few attributes as they pleased.

friendships. "If you are just liked," says one, "there is very little you cannot do in this House."

The degree to which friendship *alone* may alter the cue diffusion process is open to question. Clearly most members believe that it does have sufficient import to justify considerable effort in their personal relations with their colleagues. Since friendship is associated with other attributes such as similar views or similar constituencies, it might be argued that it has little independent effect in determining who will give cues to whom. Presumably members become friends from being on the same side of many issues. Thus, when a member takes a cue from a friend, he is only doing what he would have done anyhow. However members do volunteer personal friendship as a criterion for cue-taking, and it is indisputable that friendships do cross attitudinal and party lines. Members sometimes form friendships during previous service in state legislatures, serve together in various work groups in the House, go on congressional junkets together, or become neighbors in Georgetown, and these associations can be quite independent of partisan or ideological concerns.

> . . . I never downplay the influence that a friend will have on your vote. I
> think this happens with all members of a legislative body. . . . I've seen it
> in the state legislature and I can see it here, in terms of the way people
> vote. You come in—you can see the man come in off the floor. He comes
> in, in a hurry, and he doesn't really know what the question is. So he
> goes up to someone he knows, and he says, "How do I vote?"

Trust

> Other members say, "Hey Joe, what's this all about?" Or they can go
> like this (thumbs up) or like that (thumbs down) across the room. A guy's
> got to have a long-lot of faith in that guy over there. . . .

Predictably, trustworthiness is a frequently mentioned attribute of cue-
givers. Seventy-two percent of our respondents mentioned it as an attribute of cue-givers; it accounted for 39 percent of all attributes mentioned. What members mean by trustworthiness varies, but all the
meanings revolve around complying with the congressional norm of
not relaying false or misleading impressions.

> Your personal integrity in the House is absolutely vital. We are all
> politicians and we all share the same code of honesty. Break it and you
> might as well not be here. . . . You can always interpret the facts as you
> wish, and that's understood. But if you misrepresent those facts in a
> situation to a colleague, you've destroyed your personal credibility.

"I think this is one of the things that you learn to respect," another
member adds. "I've never had a member give me false information."
A member can mislead a colleague by advising him to vote in a way
that is contrary either to the latter's principles or to his constituency
interest. Those who avoid such misleading advice rapidly develop
reputations as being trustworthy sources of information. It is not
uncommon for vigorous advocates of bills to advise colleagues in the
cloakroom that a vote for their bill might be inconsistent with the
member's voting record, or harmful for his reelection.

"Well I make it a point, and always have, to seek out those who are closely connected with the decision," says one member.

> And I ask them—and I usually try to seek out somebody that is a personal friend of mine; somebody I'm on not a political but a friendship basis (with), so that I can turn and say, "Now give me, even though you are for this thing, give me the pros and cons of it." Somebody I trust would do that.

Another way in which members can mislead their colleagues is to advise them on the basis of insufficient study. With legislative study time at a premium, that is not uncommon. Those who have done their homework thoroughly develop invaluable reputations for trustworthiness. "I think the only way I've seen anybody in the legislative body gain the respect of his colleagues," comments one member, "is to do his homework. . . . The gadflies, the ones that want to talk on everything, lose respect or never get any respect."

Similar Views

Everyone is in favor of taking advice from those with sound judgment, and the definition of sound judgment usually boils down to, "He votes the way I do." "Of course . . . you must deal with a person in whom you have confidence," a Southern Democrat says, "and not only in his reporting correctly, but also in his being a sound thinker and having the proper approach." This criterion makes sense; for who is better qualified to estimate a member's preference than another member who agrees with him on most other issues?

Similar views and voting records accounted for 36 percent of all attributes of cue-givers mentioned during our interviews. Sixty-six percent of our respondents mentioned it. Clearly an important variable in shaping the nature of the cue-taking structure, it is at the same time an explanation of the fact that a decision-making theory based on cue-taking will make largely the same predictions as an ideological decision-making framework. *Cue-taking is the operational mechanism that translates similar attitudes into similar votes.*

Frequently the very definition of the nature of an issue is based on who is for it and who is against it. In the bitter struggle over the Nixon Administration's Voting Rights Bill, James Corman (Dem., Cal.) commented on the floor of the House:

> I would like to say to those who question whether there is any real dif-
> ference in these two bills, all I ask is for them to look at the players
> today. Look at who is supporting the administration bill and look at who
> is supporting the continuation of the existing voting rights law. One can-
> not in good conscience have any question left about what he will do if he
> believes in protecting the rights of American citizens.[2]

The issue was clear without reading the long and complex bill. Virtually all the Southerners supported the Nixon bill, and virtually all
the traditional civil rights forces opposed it.

When a member has to make a decision on a bill or resolution
about which he knows very little, basing his vote on cues provided by
those members who vote as he does when he does have sufficient information is a reasonable procedure, leading to dependable results.

Reciprocity

"You know you can't go around taking information from (other
members) all the time without giving them information." The giver of
information provides a service to its recipient. The receiver of the cue
is obligated to develop his own expertise in some area, and return the
service by advising others in his policy area.

Fourteen percent of our respondents mentioned reciprocity in
describing their cue-taking situations, representing eight percent of all
the attributes of cue-givers volunteered by the congressmen we talked
to. We expect that reciprocal cue-taking is considerably more
widespread than these figures suggest. Many members do it so automatically that they don't think to mention it. Members of Republican
sociolegislative groups (Wednesday Club, SOS, Chowder and Marching Society, Acorns, and others), for instance, regularly meet for the

purpose of swapping advice in their respective areas of expertise. Class groups and state party delegations frequently engage in similar behavior. But such institutionalized reciprocity is considered later. Here our concern is with the willingness to reciprocate as a mutual attribute of cue-givers and cue-takers.

These attributes are necessary, but not sufficient, for defining the group of initial individual cue-givers. Having them is not sufficient to be a cue-giver if the member has not made a decision at an early date that can be viewed as a cue by other members. Usually this requires that the member occupy one of several formal positions in the House.

THE POSITIONS OF INITIAL CUE-GIVERS

Along with personal qualities, legislative positions determine who will be cue-givers. Some permit, or even require, early decisions. Others provide their incumbents with more information than ordinary members have on specific subjects. Thus, when asked to describe their cue-givers, many members answered in positional terms.

The Reporting Committee

Table 5-2 reasserts the often noted importance of legislative committees in the House. Eighty-six percent of our respondents mentioned committee members as cue-givers. "No one knows any more about a piece of legislation than those who heard the arguments in committee," comments one member, and there is pretty general agreement on that point. Even those who oppose committee recommendations sometimes admit that they deal from a position of weakness. A foe of high military spending told of one encounter with L. Mendel Rivers, then Chairman of the Armed Services Committee:

> I'll never forget one year we had a Vietnam War appropriation, and I went up to Mendel Rivers and said, "Mendel, you know I usually go along with you," which, of course, he knows is a bad joke, "but," I said,

"somehow on this one I just can't do it. So," I said, "on this one I'm going to speak against this thing, but I'm not going to yield to you, because
you know more about this subject matter area than I do, and I'm not going to have my people back home able to recognize that by getting into
some kind of back and forth debate." Mendel's response was, "You don't
yield to me, and you don't yield to anybody." The next speaker after
me—who obviously didn't do this—he wasn't on his feet 15 seconds and
Mendel was demanding that he yield. And when you yield, he can put in
the record, God knows what, by way of buttressing the point he's making. He's got this enormous staff and military establishment behind him
and, reading the debate, he can make you look like an idiot.

The committee collectively and its members individually are potent
cue-givers for the obvious reason of expertise. Their recommendations
also have a legitimacy that is not possessed by noncommittee experts.
"I think the whole committee structure depends," comments a
member, "on depending on committees. If you have to challenge the

TABLE 5-2   POSITIONS OF INITIAL CUE-GIVERS, BY PARTY (PERCENT
OF ALL POSITION MENTIONS)[a]

	Position				
Party	Committee Member	Committee Chairman	Committee Ranking Minority Member	Party Leader	Total
Democrats	36	32	7	25	100 (n = 95)
Republicans	37	12	25	25	99 (n = 122)
All members	36	21	18	25	100 (N = 217)

[a] The number of position mentions exceeds the number of respondents
because members were free to mention as many or few positions as they
pleased.

conclusions of the committees as a normal rule, you're going to have chaos."

Forty-five percent of the sample mentioned committee chairmen as cue-givers. That twice as many Democrats as Republicans look to chairmen should not obscure the fact that significant numbers in both parties are interested in the chairman's position. Ranking minority members do as well as cue-givers in their own party as do the chairmen, but do not frequently serve as cue-givers for members on the other side of the aisle. In the Democratically controlled Ninety-first Congress, 30 percent of the Republicans in the sample mentioned the chairman, while only 14 percent of the Democrats said they looked to ranking minority members. The two key committee positions combined account for over 38 percent of all mentions of cue-givers; somewhat more than all other committee members (36 percent).

These figures probably exaggerate the dominance of the chairman and the ranking member in the cue-giving structure. Examination of individual responses shows that the chairman and ranking member are frequently mentioned as guides to the nature of the issue, whose positions should be known but not necessarily followed: "I just assume that I would want to know (the position of) the committee chairman," a Democrat said, "but this wouldn't mean I wouldn't vote against it." A Republican makes a similar comment about the senior member of his party, "I'd have to say the ranking minority member of the reporting committee would give me a lot of information, (but) you don't necessarily follow (it)."

In most cases there is only one chairman and one ranking minority member to follow. It is not surprising that few members are willing to accept their evaluations automatically, for the likelihood that these two men will share similar views and other common attributes with many cue-takers is small. Cue-takers can pick and choose among the whole committee membership to find members whose attributes are most suitable. "I go to a person on the committee whom I trust," says one member, "and whose views are more or less synonymous with mine." "Every member will have someone on every committee," comments another, "with whom he has a close personal relationship, or . . . confidence. We'll talk with those members on the committee in whom we have the most respect and confidence and work it out."

The cues given by rank and file committee members are more likely to be accepted, because they are sought by members who have reason to trust the source.

> Say you are not a member of the committee, and you don't know too much about this legislation; you see a friend on the floor who you know was on the committee. You might ask his opinion real quick, "What do you think of this bill? Do you think it's a good bill or do you not?" Because he's heard the hearings. You know how he votes. You know whether he's a liberal, moderate, or conservative. And you maybe know by his past voting record that he more or less would express an opinion very similar to yours. So you have confidence in his opinion, and thereby derive a decision on the bill.

The cue from the rank and file committee member will thus frequently be a pure evaluation—the answer to the question, "How should I vote?" Pure evaluation requires little communication, and need not be face-to-face.The cue-taker can learn what he wants to know simply by watching his cue-giver vote on the floor, or by asking someone else how the cue-giver voted.

The opportunity for a committee member to give a cue that is independent of the "committee position" is a function of the internal unity of the committee. Members may give cues by supporting the committee position as well as by opposing it, of course. But the value of a message is low if the information is redundant.

Party Leaders

The role of party leaders in the diffusion structure is particularly difficult to analyze because of the wide variation in their behavior.[3] They are individuals, like the initial cue-givers, but sometimes they speak for groups or for the President of the United States. Particularly when they are of the President's party, their positions on legislative issues may be established early in the legislative process, thus putting them squarely in the "initial cue-giver" category. Other times their decisions may be reached midway in the process, influencing, with or without intent, later cue-takers. Finally, they can and sometimes do make decisions on the basis of cues at the final stage of the diffusion process. It is almost tautological to assert that their time of decision is related to the degree of partisanship of the issue, for one of the components of what we normally think of as a partisan issue is that leaders of the two parties have staked out public positions early in the process.

Be that as it may, party leaders account for 25 percent of all mentions of individual cue-givers. Probably, as with committee leaders, the positions of party leaders are often considered a datum that should be known, and even considered, but not necessarily *the* basis for a decision. A somewhat greater proportion of Republicans (62 percent) than Democrats (48 percent) said that they looked to party leadership for voting cues.

THE INTERMEDIARIES

When confronted with the necessity of making a quick low-information decision on legislation, members of the House can follow one of two courses. They can look to the initial cue-givers, individuals who have made up their minds early and are perceived to be experts. Usually, as demarcated above, these are members of the standing committee that reported the measure to the floor. Sometimes they are party leaders or individuals who have developed a reputation for expertise without holding relevant committee or party positions. Or they can look to intermediate cue-givers—groups of members who have evaluated the cues from initial decision-makers and arrived at a collective position. Sometimes, of course, these intermediate groups fail to arrive at anything approaching a consensus view on the matter in question. Then the undecided member obtains little aid or comfort from them; a sharply and evenly divided intermediate group tells the undecided member only that the issue is controversial among those

colleagues with whom he would like to identify. But when intermediate groups have a clearly preponderant view, undecided and ill-
informed members are likely to go along with the crowd.

When asked whose position they would like to know in a
hypothetical voting situation where they could know nothing else, the
members of the House we interviewed were a little more likely to
choose groups that normally operate in intermediary roles than ac-
knowledged experts (Table 5-3).[4] Intermediate cue-givers are thus

TABLE 5-3   MEMBERS' CHOICE OF CUE-GIVERS IN A HYPOTHETICAL
"ZERO-INFORMATION" SITUATION[a]

Initial Cue-Givers	Number of Mentions	Percent of All Mentions
Chairman	34	13
Ranking minority member	29	11
President	35	14
All initial cue-givers	98	39
Intermediary Cue-Givers		
State party delegation	44	18
Party majority	19	7
Majority of the House	9	4
Democratic Study Group or Wednesday Club	32	13
"Conservative Coalition"	12	5
All intermediary cue-givers	116	46
Not Classified		
Party leaders	40	16
Total	254	101

[a] Members were allowed to choose from zero to three cue-givers from the
list of 10. Democratic Study Group and Wednesday Club were separate
choices, combined here for analysis.

more than a theoretical possibility, they are a major part of the cue-diffusion process as it exists in the House of Representatives.

One reason for the importance of intermediary cue-givers seems to be the quite small number of members who make initial decisions about most legislative proposals. This relative handful of initial cue-givers frequently lacks the requisite bases of influence to pass authoritative cues to *all* members of the House without the intervention of intermediaries. Expertise accounts for only one-third of all bases for cues mentioned in our interviews;[5] and expertise more than anything else is the basis of the initial cue-givers' claim to be followed (Table 5-4). Most members seem to prefer to take cues from sources with *several* perceived bases of influence—expertise, plus reference, plus legitimacy, for example. This means the small group of initial decision-makers and cue-givers must be expanded outward if it is to provide cues from sources with the requisite number and type of influence bases for *all* members of the House to reach a low-information decision. The successive addition of intermediaries to the central group adds new influence bases (especially reference and legitimacy) to the claim of the initially active experts.

Party Leaders

The most striking thing about intermediary groups in the House of Representatives is their partisan character; most of the major channels from center to periphery as cues diffuse outward are party-oriented reference groups.

The intermediary role of party leaders in the House has already been mentioned. Accounting for 16 percent of all mentions of cue-givers, the leaders clearly play a major role in shaping the outward spread of evaluations. "Whenever possible," comments a Southern Democrat, "I attempt to accommodate the leadership of the party." And this comment is a typical one for members of both parties from all regions. Most members feel duty bound to ascertain the views of their party leaders and go along in the absence of contrary inclinations.

TABLE 5-4 BASES OF INFLUENCE ATTRIBUTED TO CUE-GIVERS,
          BY PARTY (PERCENT)[a]

		Influence Base			
	Expertise	Reference	Legitimacy	Reward/ Coercion	Total
Democrats	35	34	21	9	99 (n = 105)
Republicans	31	32	27	10	100 (n = 112)
All members	33	33	24	9	99 (N = 217)

[a] The number of bases coded for each member varied from zero to four.

Such contrary inclinations might be based, in addition to independently derived views, on the cues of more immediate and potent sources.

Journalistic accounts frequently point to reward and coercion as the basis for the influence of party leaders. The members that we interviewed do not, for the most part, see it in those terms:

> This is the thing that I think is most important—what the leadership is in a position to do for you and against you is just, frankly, so marginal and limited . . . relative to what you have to do for yourself [that] after you've been here for a few terms they reach, for whatever reasons [the conclusion], that they need you more than you need them. . . . It's true vis-à-vis the White House, and I think it's true internally here in the House.

Members refer repeatedly to the *legitimate* role of the Party leader as cue-giver; he is elected to look after the interests of the party, and when he performs that function he has a legitimate right to make recommendations. Members, even those who frequently vote against party stands, recognize a common stake in the image projected by ac-

tions of the congressional party and feel a responsibility to strengthen
the party position, whenever doing so does not conflict with their individual needs.

The influence of party is also apparent when the congressional
party acts as a *reference group* for individual members in search of
cues. If party leaders have influence based on legitimacy, party majorities have a natural reference base. "I would also respect the position of the majority of my party," says a Republican, "because it
would embrace a political philosophy which I would respect." In this
way the party as a reference group serves to translate ideology into the
decisions of its members.

The State Party Delegation

There is good reason to suspect that the state party delegation is a
potent source of cues. It has a reference base—in most cases it is
probably stronger than the national party as a reference group—and is
at the same time a means of estimating constituency interests. Particularly if the member's decision strategy is one of minimizing regrets
(rather than maximizing satisfaction), the protective coloration of voting with state party colleagues is invaluable:

> . . . you all face generally the same kind of an electorate. You know the
> local newspaper; you know the local situation; you can weigh the impact
> of a particular vote together. And this is a comforting thing to know that
> a guy who faces the same sort of people you do—who reads the same
> newspaper [and] has the same factors influencing him—that he comes
> out the same way you do. The other major factor of course is the factor of
> trying to be consistent. You can always be whipsawed by an opponent if
> you vote differently from your Democratic colleagues. He says, "My
> God, friend, even this man's colleagues had enough sense to vote this
> way, but he went the other direction." Unity for strength! If the whole
> delegation gets together on an issue you're less likely to be criticized.

The danger of spuriousness in asserting the primary role of the
delegation as cue-giver is great, combining as it does a number of fac-

tors that would lead to a prediction of highly correlated voting records within the group in the absence of cue-taking. The interviews are thus particularly crucial evidence on this point. Table 5-3 tends to confirm the hypothesized major role of the state delegation. It collectively, or its members individually, is *the most frequently mentioned cue-giver*, representing 18 percent of all mentions of cue-givers and 38 percent of all mentions of intermediaries.

The behavior of delegations is difficult to describe. There is no single pattern—variation in the type and frequency of internal interaction is extensive. The size of the delegation, its distance from "home," its political homogeneity, and the inclinations and energy of its dean all affect the behavior of the group. Some large delegations have regular formal meetings (California and Texas Democrats, Michigan Republicans), and some virtually never assemble (New York Democrats). Small delegations seldom have formal meetings, but sustain a high level of interaction on the floor and at social occasions.

Two sorts of factors seem to be at work in bolstering the cue-giving capability of state delegations. In the smaller delegations members find it easy to compare notes before they vote—and politically important to do so.

> We meet regularly from time to time on legislation (and) if at all possible, we try to vote alike, particularly my colleague from_____, because it does at times become annoying when newspapers pick up the number of times we vote differently, coming from the same metropolitan area—the same constituency. Newspapers thrive on differences. They will never refer to the times we vote alike on legislation, but two or three times in a row on opposite sides of a vote—they immediately have a story.

In large delegations the "defensive advantage"[6] of cohesive voting may be less important, but another factor makes for strong internal cue-taking; the delegation itself may make a conscious attempt to serve as an all-purpose diffusion mechanism. Large delegations disperse their members as widely as possible across policy areas (hence committees) and make an attempt to have an "expert" within the delegation who can inform (and give cues to) the rest of the delegation on all legislation:

> Well, being from Pennsylvania, I'll use that as an example. There are 13
> Republicans from Pennsylvania, and we meet about once every three
> weeks. I think we are on 13 different committees, but each member briefs
> the other members on legislation that is forthcoming from his commit-
> tee. . . . And I find it useful. . . .

Where this "going round the table" is not formalized in a delegation
meeting, it may occur with no less effect on the floor.

Members of small delegations are forced to look outside of the delegation for expertise; frequently they find it in sociolegislative groups,
which in some ways are functional alternatives to the state delegation.

Sociolegislative Groups

At least on the formal level, the small sociolegislative group is a pecu-
liarly Republican institution. In its typical form it has about as many
members as there are committees. It operates like the large state party
delegation; its regular meetings serve as mutual briefing sessions, with
each member passing on information and cues in his area of
competence:

> I'm a member of two different Republican sociolegislative groups, the
> SOS Club and the Chowder and Marching Society. . . . Part of the pur-
> pose of these groups is to go around the room and have each member talk
> about the status of legislation pending before his committee. I am af-
> forded the opportunity on a regular systematized basis, twice each week,
> to discuss with my colleagues legislation pending before virtually every
> one of the committees of the House.

The Republican groups do not, for the most part, attempt to act as
cue-givers for nonmembers; one that does is notoriously unsuccessful
according to our respondents. They exist to serve the information
needs of their members, avoiding publicity to facilitate free interchange
within the group.

The influence of the Republican groups in the diffusion of cues is probably great. Because their pervasiveness was not fully appreciated in the early stages of our research, that influence remains poorly measured. Thirty-eight percent of the Republicans in the sample volunteered information about membership in such groups; if they had been directly questioned about group membership, the figure would be higher. It is probably safe to estimate that well over half of the Republicans in the House belong to such groups.

The structure and functions of party-oriented intermediaries on the Democratic side are considerably different from their Republican counterparts. The Democratic Study Group (DSG) exists mainly as an instrument for attaining policy goals, not to serve the day-to-day needs of its members, although it does some of that too.[7] It is more an action group than a discussion group—it's much too large for the kind of informal discussions that are the stock-in-trade of the Republican groups. It seeks to fulfill a leadership function both for its members and, unlike the Republican groups, for nonmembers. Frequently an intermediary, the DSG, through its task forces, sometimes serves as an initial cue-giver where the House committee structure is heavily stacked against liberal positions. The DSG staff and its leaders can be counted upon to screen the voting cues of initial cue-givers and reflect and reinforce the liberal ones:

> If it were a broad issue of national policy, and I don't know anything about the bill, I would think that the Study Group's position would have the most influence on me; because I'm involved in it. I generally end up at the same place as most of the other fellows. The research is good. There's a blending of a lot of good ideas.

By rough count 62 percent of our Democratic sample belong to the DSG. But belonging to the DSG is a matter of degree: there are many who are on the mailing list who do not "belong"; formal members are involved in it in varying degrees. It is an inclusive organization, unlike the Republican groups where membership is sharply defined, and the DSG does not discourage members who are considerably more conservative than the DSG norm from maintaining a fringe association. Its influence is debated, but it is certain that many members use it as a reference—both positive and negative. Its informal positions define "liberal" and "conservative" for the member who doesn't wish to study a bill.

Finally, in both parties there are ad hoc reference groups that carry considerable weight in the informal dissemination of cues. They are composed of members who normally vote together for a variety of reasons, and because they normally vote together they come to value the opinions of one another. They are the "good guys":

> I came out of the Democratic Cloakroom, and we were having a vote. . . . You know frequently our friends from New Jersey, New York, Michigan, and California, the Northern Democrats—of course, we think we're the good guys. And we'll always say, "What are the good guys doing?" Well I walked out of the cloakroom this one day to the rear of the chamber over on the right, on the Democratic side, which is sort of the place that the Southern Democrats tend to sit and congregate. As I walked up the three steps there and started down the aisle, I overheard this conversation in a deep Southern drawl, and this fellow said, "What are the good guys doing on this one?" So the "good guy" is in the eye of the beholder.

Nonpartisan Intermediaries

While the diffusion of cues from the initial decision-makers to the entire membership of the House is dominated by party-related intermediaries, at least two nonpartisan agencies sometimes play a role in this process.

One of these is the full committee reporting a measure to the floor. Although practice varies from committee to committee, subcommittees are important in most.[8] Where subcommittees make the initial policy decision, when the committee attempts no independent assessment of the issue but, with little or no internal division, accepts the subcommittee's recommendations as its own, the committee consensus can serve as an intermediate cue. The members of the House we interviewed seldom mentioned committee consensus as a cue—perhaps because they were less interested in the position of the entire committee than in a few selected members, or perhaps because they found such conflict-free decision-making uninteresting. But united committees tend to get their way on the floor, nonetheless.

Similarly, the preponderant opinion of the House as a whole was seldom mentioned as a cue in our interviews (only 4 percent of all mentions). Yet members do care what their colleagues of both parties think of legislation. "I would be influenced by the feeling, and that is difficult to describe," says one member, "the temper of the body that day, the temper of the House, the attitude of all the members toward it. . . . I would certainly like to have the feel of the temper of the House, which comes down to the attitude of the majority of the members." That this feeling was not confined to the respondent quoted above is suggested by the fact that the records of a handful of members do not indicate a single instance in which they voted against a majority of their colleagues!

WHO TAKES CUES FROM WHOM?

The end result of the diffusion of cues is that members of the House of Representatives are able to make low-information decisions about how to vote on the floor in which they can have considerable confidence. While the decision rule of the members is simple, the process that makes it possible for virtually all members to vote on the basis of cues from their colleagues is complex. We have sought, in the immediately preceding pages, to describe some of the main characteristics of that process. As we have seen, members of the House (and especially those who make up their minds late in the game) often can choose between a large number and variety of cue sources. Who, then, tends to take cues from whom? Our interviews permit us to suggest some partial and preliminary answers.

Again, we must rely on the members' responses to questioning about their probable behavior in a hypothetical low-information vot-ing situation (Appendix A Question 14). They were presented with a list of possible cue-givers and asked which individuals' or groups' positions they would like to know. Their responses allow us to sketch portraits of the influence networks of the cue-givers on the list (although, of course, not of any others). These portraits are complex. The number of variables related to the choice of cue-giver is obviously large, and none of these variables is fully independent of the others. All this suggests more than usual scholarly caution in interpreting these results.

In order to simplify matters somewhat, we describe the clientele of each of the nine cue-givers by looking at those categories of members who overselected (compared to the norm for all members) and underselected the cue. We examine those individuals and groups who usually serve as initial cue-givers first, and then examine the clienteles of the intermediaries.

The Clienteles of Initial Cue-Givers

Party leaders function at some times as initial cue-givers and at other times as intermediaries. For present purposes we have lumped them into the first category. They prove to be the most popular of the four initial cue-givers; 46 percent of the members indicated that they would like to know the position of their party leaders in the House if they knew nothing else about a bill (Table 5-5).

The existence of an active state party delegation appears to be an alternative source of information and evaluation which limits the influence of party leaders in these low-information situations; members with especially active delegations underselect party leaders as cue sources whereas those with average or less interaction with their delegation overselect them. The sociolegislative groups, in many ways equivalent to the state delegations, do *not* seem to serve the same function. Rather, members of the DSG and the Republican discussion groups apparently constitute the hard core of support for their respective party leaders. Members who report an unusually large number of legislative specialties are relatively recalcitrant to party leadership cues, perhaps because of the unusually high value these members place

TABLE 5-5   WHO TAKES CUES FROM WHICH INITIAL CUE-GIVERS?

	Percentage of Group Mentioning Cue-Giver	Deviation from House Norm	N
PARTY LEADERS	46		(87)
Groups overselecting cue			
State delegation interaction av. or less [17][a]	63	+17	(38)
Sociolegislative group member	60	+14	(47)
Groups underselecting cue			
Many specialties (4 or more) [1]	20	−26	(15)
Active state delegation [17]	30	−16	(30)
Not sociolegislative group member	30	−16	(40)
THE PRESIDENT	40		(87)
Groups overselecting cue			
Low-seniority members (1–2 Terms)	57	+17	(23)
Nonideological orientation [21]	54	+14	(41)
Groups underselecting cue			
Ideologues [21]	28	−12	(32)

on subject-matter expertise. (This same group tends to overselect committee chairmen and underselect party and House majorities as cue sources.)

The second most popular initial cue-giver was the President of the United States; 40 percent of the members indicated that they would like to know his position. Curiously, the President was not *voluntarily* mentioned as a source of cues often throughout the remainder of the interviews. This suggests, to us at least, that the President's position on legislative proposals helps define the nature of the issue to congressmen more than it serves as an authoritative evaluation for them. In a situation of nearly total ignorance, members find it handy to know where the President stands, especially (but not only) if the

TABLE 5-5   (Continued)

	Percentage of Group Mentioning Cue-Giver	Deviation from House Norm	N
CHAIRMAN OF REPORTING COMMITTEE	39		(87)
Groups overselecting cue			
No contact with state delegation [16]	67	+28	(9)
Democrats	56	+17	(45)
Not sociolegislative group member	55	+16	(40)
Many specialties (4 or more) [1]	53	+14	(15)
Age, 60+	50	+11	(39)
High-seniority members (8+ terms)	47	+ 8	(19)
Groups underselecting cue			
Republican sociolegislative group members	12	−27	(17)
Nonideological orientation [21]	27	−12	(41)
Unaffiliated Republicans	28	−11	(25)
COMMITTEE RANKING MINORITY MEMBER	33		(87)
Groups overselecting cue			
Unaffiliated Republicans	72	+39	(25)
Republican sociolegislative group members	53	+20	(17)
Only one specialty [1]	53	+20	(19)
Low-seniority members (1–2 terms)	48	+15	(23)
Specializes in committee work only [1, 2]	44	+11	(41)
Groups underselecting cue			
Democratic Study Group members	3	−30	(30)
Unaffiliated Democrats	20	−13	(15)
Active state delegation [17]	23	−10	(30)

[a] Numbers in brackets are question numbers where classifications are based on interview responses.

President is of the congressman's party. This, however, may have relatively little to do with how they vote.

Low-seniority congressmen markedly overselected the presidency as a cue-giver. At least three explanations of this finding are plausible: (1) the junior members were mostly Republicans reacting to a Republican president; (2) congressmen who were new to Capitol Hill had yet fully to learn the internal cue-giving and cue-taking system or the identity of congressional experts, and hence opted to follow the highly visible presidency; and (3) the electoral vulnerability of junior members lead them to huddle under the protective wing of the presidency. All of these, of course, could be simultaneously true. But the fact that the junior members also overselected ranking minority members as cue-givers lends greater weight to the first two explanations.

A second category of House member—this one defined in attitudinal terms—also overselected the president. Those members who said that ideology rarely played a part in their decision-making overselected the president as cue-giver, while their opposite numbers underselected him. Again, alternative explanations of this finding can be argued.

A large number of groups distinctively over- or underselect the committee chairmen as cue-givers. Explanations for some of these are easy but trivial. Committee chairmen in the Ninety-first Congress tended to be aging, high-seniority Democrats; the same categories of members tended to overselect them as cue-givers. Nor is it surprising that committee chairmen were underselected by Republicans. More interesting, however, are the figures that suggest that a tendency to turn to committee chairmen as cue-givers depends on the availability of alternative sources of information and evaluation. Congressmen who reported no contact with their state party delegations (in some cases because they had none) or who were *not* members of any sociolegislative group heavily overselected the chairman as a source of voting cues. Indeed, Republicans who belong to sociolegislative groups were the least likely of all members to take cues from the chairmen. That only part of this distinctiveness results from differences in party affiliation can be seen by examining the unaffiliated Republicans. They underselected the committee chairmen, too, but far less so. Finally, members who seem to place an unusually high value on individual legislative expertise (by claiming four or more areas of expertise themselves) also turned to committee chairmen for policy guidance with unusual frequency.

Patterns of response to the committee ranking minority member again illustrate the significance of alternative cue sources. Republicans overselect the ranking member from their side, but those who are unaffiliated are far more likely to do so than those who can turn to sociolegislative groups for alternative Republican cues. Democrats underselect the ranking member; those belonging to the Democratic Study Group most dramatically so. With Democrats there is also an ideological explanation for the divergence between group members and nonmembers; nonmembers are disproptionately drawn from the conservative end of the Democratic spectrum, and hence more likely than DSG members to sympathize with the views of Republican committee leaders.

The state party delegation again appears as an alternative information source, with members of both parties who report frequent delegation interaction underselecting the ranking minority member.

The Clienteles of Intermediary Cue-Givers

The state party delegation was the most frequently mentioned source of cues—be they "initial" or "intermediate"—and its impact was relatively uniform across the various subgroups within the House. However, the amount of interaction within the delegation does matter. Members from active delegations tend to overselect them as cue sources; those from relatively inactive delegations mention them less often (Table 5-6). Membership in a sociolegislative group, at least on the Republican side, provides an alternative source of information and evaluation that seems to result in an underselection of the delegation as a cue-giver. Finally, those members of the House whose legislative interests are confined solely to their committee work seem to lean more heavily on their delegations for policy guidance than others do. The

TABLE 5-6   WHO TAKES CUES FROM INTERMEDIATE CUE-GIVERS?

	Percentage of Group Mentioning Cue-Giver	Deviation from House Norm	N
STATE PARTY DELEGATION	51	—	(87)
Groups overselecting cue			
Active state delegation [17]	67	+16	(30)
Specializes in committee work only [1, 2]	61	+10	(41)
Groups underselecting cue			
Republican sociolegislative group members	41	−10	(17)
State delegation interaction av. or less [17]	42	− 9	(38)
DEMOCRATIC STUDY GROUP	31	—	(87)
Groups overselecting cue			
Democratic Study Group members	80	+49	(30)
Ideologues [21]	41	+10	(32)
Groups underselecting cue			
Republicans	5	−26	(42)
Unaffiliated Democrats	7	−24	(15)
Low-Seniority members (1–2 terms)	13	−18	(23)
Age, 60+	14	−17	(14)
High-seniority members (8+ terms)	16	−15	(19)

other side of the coin of highly focused legislative interests is the need to trust the advice of colleagues most of the time. Quite possibly such trust leads to narrow specialization rather than vice versa.

The Democratic Study Group and the "Conservative coalition" may be treated as mirror images of one another. Not surprisingly, DSG members prominently overselect the DSG and underselect the "Conservative coalition." Older members and those with the greatest accumulation of seniority underselect the DSG and overselect the "Con-

TABLE 5-6   (Continued)

	Percentage of Group Mentioning Cue-Giver	Deviation from House Norm	N
PARTY MAJORITY	22	—	(87)
Groups overselecting cue			
Low education	40	+18	(10)
Groups underselecting cue			
Many specialties (4 or more) [1]	7	− 15	(15)
Low-seniority members (1–2 terms)	13	− 9	(23)
CONSERVATIVE COALITION	14	—	(87)
Groups overselecting cue			
Age, 60 +	36	+22	(14)
High seniority (8 + terms)	26	+12	(19)
Ideologues [21]	22	+ 8	(32)
Groups underselecting cue			
Democratic Study Group members	7	− 7	(30)
HOUSE MAJORITY	10	—	(87)
Groups overselecting cue			
Age, 60 +	21	+11	(14)
Only one specialty [1]	21	+11	(19)
Groups underselecting cue			
Many specialties (4 or more) [1]	0	− 10	(15)

servative coalition." Prominently underselecting the DSG are also Republicans, unaffiliated Democrats (mostly from the South), and the lowest seniority group, which is itself mostly Republican. None need explanation.

What the DSG and the "Conservative coalition" have in common is the attention, as attested to by overselection, of those with ideological orientations. For those who see legislation as a contest over ideological principles, the "right" and "wrong" positions tend to be defined by these two cue-givers. Not a few of these ideological members say they look to *both* groups for cues, to verify both that the "good guys" are for a bill and the "bad guys" against it.

The final two intermediate cue-givers on our list were both "bandwagon" cues—the party majority and the House majority. Both were selected by so few members that explanation is hazardous. However the data suggest that those most likely to respond to bandwagon cues are older, less educated, and more narrowly specialized than most. Those who place an unusually high value on expertise (claiming four or more areas of special knowledge for themselves) and junior members may be less likely to go along with the herd.

SUMMARY AND CONCLUSIONS

We began this chapter with a very simple theory of decision-making in the House of Representatives. When required to cast a yea or nay vote on an issue about which they knew very little—the "normal" voting situation for most members—congressmen follow cues from their colleagues. Although the theory adequately depicts the process of final choice of individual members, it tells us rather little about the processes of collective choice and fails to provide answers to a number of other basic questions. In order to compensate for some of these limitations we added greater complexity to the model by distinguishing between initial and intermediate cue-givers and introducing a variety of different bases upon which cues could be accepted. These modifications made it possible, at least in theory, to explain the diffusion of cues from a small set of initial decision-makers to the entire membership.

Models, by definition, are highly simplified versions of reality. Even after introducing these modifications, our theory was rather simple. But was it congruent with the real world? The large part of this chapter was devoted to a report on what members of Congress *say* about the diffusion of cues and how they choose between alternative ones. On the whole our respondents in the House presented a picture consistent with our theory. They were able to add much descriptive detail to the bare bones of our abstract speculations. We were thus able to describe the personal attributes cue-takers look for in initial cue-givers and the kinds of formal positions the latter characteristically occupy. The characteristics of intermediate cue-givers—to whom undecided members are more likely to turn than initial cue-givers—were also discussed. Finally we were able to examine, in a preliminary fashion, the propensity of different types of congressmen to look to different cue sources for information and evaluation.

But interviews have their limitations as a means of discovering, describing, and analyzing the real world of Capitol Hill.[9] Another independent test of our theory is desirable. We report such a test in the next chapter.

NOTES

1. J. French, Jr. and B. Raven, "The Bases of Social Power," in D. Cartwright (ed.), *Studies in Social Power* (Ann Arbor: University of Michigan Press, 1959), pp. 183–220. Our use of the bases of influence notion is borrowed more directly from David Kovenock, "Influence in the U.S. House of Representatives: Some Preliminary Statistical Snapshots," Prepared for delivery at the 1967 annual meeting of the American Political Science Association; and, more recently, "Influence in the U.S. House of Representatives: A Statitistical Analysis of Communications," *American Politics Quarterly,* Vol. 1 (October 1973), pp. 407–464.

2. *Congressional Record* (Daily Edition), December 11, 1969, p. H12138.

3. For a more complete delineation of strategies and behavior of party leaders, see Randall B. Ripley, *Party Leaders in the House of Representatives* (Washington, D.C.: The Brookings Institution, 1967); and Charles O. Jones, *The Minority Party in Congress* (Boston: Little, Brown, 1970), pp. 25–54.

4. Members chose from a list of the nine cue-givers isolated in our earlier computer simulations. The Wednesday Club was added to the list, but has been deleted from the analysis since it was ignored by all but its own (small) membership. The number of cue-givers chosen from our list could vary from a minimum of none to a maximum of three. Some cautions are in order about the responses to this question. First, there are only 87 responses from our sample of 100 members. Reasons for nonresponse are: (1) the question was not asked of members who claimed that they never engaged in cue-taking. (2) Some members refused to answer any hypothetical questions (resulting in one extreme case in a flash card crumpled and thrown in the face of the interviewer). (3) Some interviews were terminated before

the question came up. (4) Some members were not asked the question in fear that an adverse reaction would terminate the interview. The 13 members for whom we have no responses tended to be considerably more senior and more conservative than the 87 who responded; hence it is reasonable to speculate that those cue-givers who tend to be picked by the senior and the conservative are more influential than our data show. Also, we remind the reader that references to cue-givers may be negative. The data that we present in the following tables are number of references, not distinguishing between positive and negative ones.

5. Coding of influence base attributions is based on a secondary review of responses to a number of interview questions. Since we did not explicitly measure attributed influence bases, coding is necessarily judgmental, and our data are accurate only in a "ball-park" sense.

6. On the notion of defensive advantage, see D. Truman, *The Congressional Party: A Case Study* (New York: Wiley, 1959), p. 258.

7. See A. Stevens, Jr., A. Miller, and T. Mann, "Mobilization of Liberal Strength in the House, 1955–1970: The Democratic Study Group," *American Political Science Review*, Vol. 68 (1974), pp. 667–681.

8. The literature on congressional committees is now vast. Some of the most notable works: R. Fenno, *Congressmen in Committees* (Boston: Little, Brown, 1973); R. Fenno, *The Power of the Purse: Appropriations Politics in Congress* (Boston: Little, Brown, 1966); and J. Manley, *The Politics of Finance: The House Committee on Ways and Means* (Boston: Little, Brown, 1970).

9. See J. Stimson, "Five Propositions About Congressional Decision-Making: An Examination of Behavioral Inferences From Computer Simulation," prepared for the Seminar on Mathematical Models of Congress, Aspen, Colorado, 1974, for a more detailed examination of the limits and weaknesses of these congressional interviews.

CHAPTER SIX

A COMPUTER SIMULATION OF CUE-TAKING

The men and women who serve in the House of Representatives have cast millions of individual recorded roll-call votes. Most of these were "normal" votes—decisions made on the basis of little information about issues of little concern to those who answered yea or nay. Each of these votes is a challenge to, and potentially a test of, the theory we have developed in the previous chapters of the book. For a theory of human behavior should result in accurate predictions about how people behave. Our theory of decision-making by congressmen is no exception.

The immense number of potential tests of our theory led to the computer as a laboratory.[1] With few exceptions,[2] our theory claims to predict all votes cast by all congressmen—be they ideological or nonideological, partisan or nonpartisan, monumental or trivial, or foreign or domestic issues. To simulate such a large number of decisions by hand would take years of tedious labor. The flashing lights and razzle-dazzle technology of computers were not needed; but their speed was.

"SIMULATION?"

Computer simulation has been widely attempted, and the number of ways it has been defined lags not far behind the number of its applications.[3] We will not join the debate about what a computer simulation either is or should be, but only stipulate how we use the word here. "Simulation" is a convenient label for our operational model; we have no other motive for using it.

There are two essential elements to our notion of simulation. One is that the simulator makes specific testable predictions of events that are unknown (but not necessarily in the future). That attribute is shared with many forms of scientific endeavor. In this case the predictions are of the form, "Member i voted Yea/Nay on roll call j." If the member actually voted, the prediction is then either right or wrong; otherwise it is ignored.[4] The event to be predicted, while "known" to the computer (i.e., contained in core storage), is unknown to the simulator (which does, however, know how cue-givers voted).

The other element of simulation—the less common one—is that the *process* followed by the simulator is analogous to that of the actor being simulated. The simulation itself can test only accuracy of prediction, but we make the twin assertion that the process the simulator follows—its program—is itself a *description* of the process of congressional decision-making.[5] Human cognitive and evaluative processes are ordinarily complex, and attempts to simulate them with a simple-minded computer are an insult to reality. But we have hypothesized an exceedingly simple behavior—forced by the multiple constraints on decision-making—susceptible to approximation by computer. The computer (properly, its program) is still far more simple-minded than the congressional decision-maker, but not so much so that it cannot engage in behavior analogous to the congressman. "Simulation" then, as we use it, means prediction of unknown events by a process analogue.

HOW ACCURATE IS "ACCURATE"?

If the structure of roll-call voting makes for difficult decisions by members—as one said, "You can't vote maybe"—it is ideal for model testing. Neither predictions nor outcomes are difficult to interpret. Votes are either Yea or Nay, and predictions are either right or wrong.[6] The natural form of aggregating our results is then in the form of batting averages: how many correct predictions out of how many total predictions?

Thus, the accuracy of our model will be measured in percentages of accurate predictions, from zero to 100. But the real baseline is not zero. Any number of simple prediction rules can make drastic improvements in accuracy from a zero baseline. A coin toss should be accurate half the time. Predicting that everyone voted Yea on every roll call would do better, probably 65 to 70 percent accurate on the average. Predicting that everyone would vote on the winning side would improve on that by a few more percentage points. These simple but theoretically useless prediction rules do not themselves establish a baseline—sophisticated models can make predictive errors on votes that come easily to simple spurious ones—but they do establish a context of expectations. Failing perfection, the judgment of the accuracy of simulations ultimately becomes a question of parsimony: how good a batting average compared to how many inputs?

Alternative criteria of accuracy are much less rigorous. Our model could be judged by how well it predicts the passage or failure of motions. Such predictions are easy for a computer simulation, particularly given the nature of its inputs, and hence not impressive. Capitol Hill journalists probably could do about as well.

A similar aggregate measure of performance is the correlation of predicted number of Yea votes with the actual number. More demanding than pass/fail predictions, this measure of accuracy is still both easy and inappropriate. It is easy because individual predictive errors cancel out. Thirty wrong Yea predictions and 20 wrong Nay predictions combined produce an impressive 10 vote net error, and in turn a high correlation coefficient. A "correlation of outcomes" criterion would be appropriate for aggregate level theories of decision-making; it is inappropriately easy for those that purport to explain individual decision-making. Individual predictions may be meaningfully aggregated, but not for the purpose of testing them.

FROM THEORY TO OPERATIONAL MODEL

The process of converting a general theory (such as the theory of cue-taking) into an operational model (a computer program) is inelegant at best. The task requires the introduction of elements that are not themselves dictated by the theory. Thus, our simulation is far more specific than our theory—it must be to make specific predictions—and it is only one of many possible operational models consistent with the theory. The gap between theory and operation is always with us. Let us look briefly at the difference between the two.

The "Normal Vote" Distinction

Our theory of congressional behavior applies only to "normal" voting situations—ones characterized by low information and low salience. Although the conceptual distinction between "normal" decisions and others is straightforward, making this distinction operationally poses unmanageable problems. It is difficult to determine how much one member knows and cares about one vote; it requires an elaborate reconstruction of the nature of the issues involved and the member's special concerns. To do so for all members on all votes is well nigh impossible. Our computer model, hence, diverges from the cue-taking theory by predicting all votes of all members, both the "normal" and the "abnormal." We can only speculate on the impact of this divergence. We think it is small, limited largely to votes of special relevance to peculiar constituency interests. On other high-information votes there is no reason to expect that members would vote against the cue-givers of their choice, chosen in large part because of similarity of views about public policy. It is precisely in these high-information situations that members can best gauge the judgment of potential cue-givers.

Assumptions

We began the construction of our operational model with a set of assumptions. Although derived from the theory of cue-taking, they are considerably more restricted and specific than the theory. They were the following:

1. The normal situation of the member of Congress with regard to most of the roll-call voting decisions he makes is one of "low information."

2. The cost of raising the member's information base to a level adequate for fully independent decisions consistent with his or her multiple goals is prohibitive, given the number, scope, and technical complexity of the decisions congressmen are expected to make.

3. Cues—pro or con evaluations of legislative issues—are available from a variety of sources (with a corresponding variety of influence bases) in the House at the time of decision.

4. Such cues are an exceedingly economical means for the member to estimate what his or her position would be if he or she had the time and information necessary for an independent decision.

5. Members vote by taking cues and develop decision strategies over time in the form of regularized hierarchies of cue-givers.

6. These strategies are influenced by such factors as ideology and constituency (and many other variables) and are, in fact, the normal process by which such causal influences are mediated into the ultimate decision.

7. Decision strategies are relatively constant across issues and over time.

These assumptions are "hypotheses" in the sense that the predictive accuracy of the simulation ultimately lends credence or undermines them. But they stand or fall as a set in the simulation, they are *not* individually "tested."[7]

Assumption number 3 presents us with an apparent paradox. We assume in the simulations that the position of every cue-giver (or at least every salient cue-giver) is known to each member in search of cues. How can we assume that cues are available information at the same time as we deny the availability of other important information? The answer lies in the ritual of the roll-call vote.

Roll-call votes are not cast simultaneously. Under the procedures followed before electronic voting was adopted in the House, members did not have to vote the first time their name was called; they could wait, watch, and listen until the clerk called their names a second time—or even longer. "Well you've got to make up (your mind) before the second go-round . . . standing in the Well," a senior Republican told us. "There have been occasions when I haven't made up my mind in a fixed manner until I go down to the Well, and I purposely hold off in order to try to accumulate a little more information, to see how the voting is going, see if maybe I'm off base." "You sometimes let a whole roll call go by," a Southerner said ". . . if there is some man you particularly admire, you sort of see how he goes the first time." The advent of electronic voting since these interviews were taken has, if anything, made the roll-call vote an even more efficient means of giving and taking cues. The members are given a period of time in which to cast their votes electronically. All pretense of voting in alphabetical order has been abandoned and each member's vote, once cast, is recorded on an electronic scoreboard. Members who choose to do so can study the patterns of voting before they, too, push the button.

Voting cues, of course, are usually available at many earlier stages in the legislative process. But if all these other opportunities have been missed or ignored, cues are alwasys available "in the last fatal moment," as one member put it, "when I have to vote." Of all the assertions we make, the safest is probably that a cue-taker can find the cue of his choice on the floor of the House at the time of the vote.

Cue-Givers Operationally Defined

Predicting past events, like shooting ducks in a pond, is not much sport without some restrictions. Without concern for parsimony or theoretical justification, only predictive perfection limits the number and variety of "refinements" that may be added to a computer model. In our model, for example, if every member were allowed to serve as a cue-giver for every other, predictions would be highly accurate but without theoretical meaning. Thus we have limited our cue-givers to nine, all institutionally defined.[8] This is one of the more important respects in which the simulation is far more specific and restricted than the theory from which it is derived. It is a price to be paid to eliminate spurious accuracy; some probably remains.[9]

The nine cue-givers in the roll-call simulations were chosen *a priori*. The choices were a combination of congressional lore and intuition. The reader searching for surprising new revelations about the sources of decision cues will be disappointed. None is new to informed congressional observers, nor to congressmen themselves, who produced essentially the same list in open-ended interviews.[10]

The essential idiocy of computers requires highly specific operational definitions of cue-givers. Computers are very good at counting and calculating, very bad at pattern recognition. Whereas individuals of mediocre intelligence can observe phenomena and "see" obvious patterns, computers see only what they are *specifically* instructed to look for. Specific often means arbitrary, and many of the parameters that make up our operational definitions of cue-givers are arbitrary. The guiding rule in all these operational decisions is that they be intuitively reasonable in the context of low-information decision-making.[11] Thus, for instance, while the computer easily discerns the existence of a majority of 50 percent + 1, the member on the floor does not; majorities (or more accurately their nuclei) must usually be larger than 50 percent to be perceptible. We turn now to a discussion of the nine cue-givers and how they were operationally defined.

PRESIDENT.   The President is the only one of our cue-givers not present on the floor at the time of the vote. His position is nonetheless well known; it appears repeatedly in debate, is discussed on the floor, and is available from the nearest doorkeeper. Data on presidential positions are from the *Congressional Almanac*.[12] Like all others, the presidential cue has three states, Yea, Nay, or Not Available.

STATE PARTY DELEGATION.   This cue is defined as "available" to a member whenever three-fourths or more of his colleagues from his state and party vote together on a roll call. The three-fourths figure is used as a cutoff on the assumption that in units as small as the State Party Delegation (the lower limit is two voting members) the mathematics of the situation can create a false impression of majority sentiment where diversity is really the case. Consider for example the four-man delegation. The member whose behavior is being observed or predicted is, of course, excluded, leaving two possible states for the other three, unanimity or a two-to-one split. A cutoff point of two thirds would define a voting cue even in the case of maximum diversity, which seems unreasonable. Again for intuitive reasons, we followed the *Congressional Quarterly* practice of breaking up some of the largest states into smaller "perceived delegations" (e.g., New York City and upstate New York) to assess the effects of this cue. We have not noted any net change in predictive accuracy from this practice.

PARTY LEADERSHIP.   A cue is considered available from the party leadership whenever the floor leader and whip of the member's *own party* vote together.[13] This cue can be given unintentionally; the two leaders may easily and frequently vote together by chance on nonparty matters. The theory of cue-taking predicts that the intentions of cue-givers are irrelevant to the member searching for a cue, and hence these chance agreements are not excluded.

COMMITTEE CHAIRMAN.   This cue is simply the vote of the chairman of the committee reporting the bill or resolution under consideration. In some committees, most particularly Appropriations, the Chairman and Ranking Member cues may be surrogates for the positions of subcommittee chairmen and ranking members. In case of votes on rules the substantive committee chairman's position is used, unless the rule itself is subject to controversy. Closed rules and rules waiving points of order are in the latter category.

RANKING MINORITY MEMBER. The position of the ranking minority member of the reporting committee is made operational in the same fashion as that of the chairman. Note that cues of the ranking member and chairman are each available to members of both parties.

CONSERVATIVE COALITION. The Conservative Coalition cue is defined when a majority of Southern Democrats votes with a majority of Midwest Republicans against a majority of non-Southern Democrats. Because all three conditions are required concurrently, and therefore presumably visibly, only 50 percent majorities are required. This version of the Conservative Coalition differs slightly from the well-known *Congressional Quarterly* definition, and indeed is only one of several that we have employed.[14]

DEMOCRATIC STUDY GROUP. Since the DSG does not take formal public positions on votes we look to the leadership element (as best we can determine it) for unanimity as a cue. Again, as we pointed out with regard to party leaders, it is not impossible for the seven leaders we use to agree without intending to give a cue.

PARTY MAJORITY. The member's party colleagues may act as a collective cue-giver if majority sentiment is clearly perceptible (two thirds or more voting together). With this and all other cues, the member's own vote is excluded from consideration when the existence and direction of cues are determined.[15]

HOUSE MAJORITY. This cue is defined when two-thirds or more of the whole membership of the House vote together. Very high levels of response to this cue are assumed to represent bandwagon tendencies.

THE MODEL

We turn now to a nontechnical description of the simulation. The model, whose program name is LEARN, is the most recent of three approaches to simulating roll-call votes we have developed. All three are consistent with the theory of cue-taking, differing in approaches to operationalization.[16]

We postulate that cue-taking is learned behavior, that members develop "cue response hierarchies" over time as they react to cue-givers on one roll call after another. These hierarchies are rough rank orderings of the cue-givers the individual member carries in his head. Because they are learned behavior, the response hierarchies are changeable over time, particularly for new members. The organization of the LEARN program is thus chronological. Taking one roll call at a time in its chronological order, the program carries out three functions for each member. The three functions are *measurement* (observation of past cue-taking behavior), *evaluation* (the determination of response hierarchies), and *prediction* of the member's vote.[17]

For member i and roll call j the measurement segment observes the member's cue-taking patterns on the 50 roll calls previous to j, or all roll calls if fewer than 50 have occured at that point in the session.[18] The effective memory of 50 votes is large enough to avoid the undue influence of a short series of strange votes, small enough to allow for genuine change of response hierarchies if it does occur.

The product of the measurement segment is, for each cue-giver, two running tallies, VWC (number of times member *voted with cue-giver*) and CAMV (number of times the *cue* was *available* and the *member* was *voting*) such that the ratio VWC/CAMV represents the proportion of agreement of member i with the cue-giver in question (number of agreements over number of opportunities). The maximum size of both numerator and denominator is 50, the proportion ranging between zero and one. The 18 tallies (VWC and CAMV for each of the nine cue-givers for member i) are the input to the evaluation segment.

For member i and roll call j the evaluation segment determines and rank orders "cue-scores." The cue-scores are determined by the formula

$$\text{Cue-Score } (k) = \frac{\text{VWC } (k)}{\text{CAMV } (k)} - .5$$

where k is a numeric code for one of the nine cue-givers.

The score is thus a simple proportion of agreement with cue-giver k minus the expected agreement by chance (.5).[19] Cue-scores may then vary between −.500 (always voted against cue-giver) and +.500 (always voted with cue-giver). Scores in the middle range indicate that the member probably ignored the cue-giver, voting with him (or it) about as often as we would expect by chance.

For the purpose of determining cue response hierarchies the program rank orders the nine scores by their *absolute values*, presumed to measure intensity of response, whether positive or negative. The evaluation segment thus produces for each member on each roll call two sorts of information that will be employed in the prediction segment, the rank order of cue-givers and the direction of response to each, positive or negative.

The prediction segment differs only in focus from measurement and evaualion. It performs one of the same tasks, ascertaining positions of cue-givers, except it does it on the current roll call, j, and instead of comparing member i's vote to the positions of cue-givers, it uses them and i's predispositions (cue-scores) to predict i's vote. It first seeks out the position of i's highest ranked cue-giver. If a cue is available from that source it determines its direction (Yea or Nay) and predicts the cue-taker's response from his predisposition (positive or negative) to that cue-giver.[20] If no cue is available from the first cue-giver, it seeks out the second, and so on until if finds an available cue for prediction. What may seem to be a complex cognitive process, evaluation, rank ordering, scanning for cues, and so forth, in reality is not, because the usual case is that the member votes with (or against) his highest ranked cue-giver and need not look at the others.

After predicting the vote the simulator scans its memory for the actual vote, compares prediction and vote, and keeps a running tally of accuracy, by member and roll call. It then moves on to member $i + 1$, and when all members have been simulated on roll call j it moves on to $j + 1$ and repeats the process.

The model is dynamic; it allows for change in cue-response patterns over time.[21] It is *not* cybernetic—there is no success/failure feedback loop that modifies future behavior—we don't believe the real-world congressman operates that way in his cue-taking behavior.

This computer model is a simplification of reality; indeed it is a simplification of the theory of cue-taking. The question is of degree. We have strongly asserted in earlier chapters that the actual decision-making process by cue-taking is quite simple. Our interviews produced independent evidence that something not unlike this model frequently occurs in the House of Representatives. So let us examine its accuracy.

RESULTS

Table 6-1 presents the performance of the LEARN program in the simplest possible terms. In the course of making about 400,000 individual predictions for the years 1965 through 1969, LEARN was right a little over 88 percent of the time. Far from perfection, that 88 percent still provides substantial support for the theory of cue-taking. Across *all* issues and for *all* members of the House, knowing nothing but the position of nine cue-givers and the cue-taking propensities of members, LEARN is right nearly 9 out of every 10 times! It is quite possible, of course, to be right for the wrong reasons and, no doubt, our simulation sometimes was. But to predict human behavior with this much accuracy, on the basis of such limited information, is rare.

Little yearly variation is evident. The range of variation for the five years simulated by LEARN is 3.0 percent, from the 89.5 percent of 1966 to the 86.5 percent of 1968. Given the enormous number of predictions underlying each yearly accuracy figure (approximately 80,000) even the most trivial percentage differences from year to year

TABLE 6-1   PREDICTIVE ACCURACY OF SIMULATIONS, BY YEAR

Year	Predictive Accuracy (percent)
1958[a]	85.7
1960[a]	86.0
1962[a]	89.3
1964[a]	87.7
1965	89.2
1966	89.5
1967	88.6
1968	86.5
1969	86.7
Average yearly accuracy	88.1
Weighted average accuracy[b]	88.1

[a] Accuracy figures for these years are based on the early SIMULATE program. They are included for reference, but not included in the averages.
[b] The weighting factor is the number of roll-call votes per year. Weighted average accuracy including the early years is 87.9 percent.

are statistically significant. But we are more impressed by the year-to-year similarity.

The differences that do appear conform to commonsense expectations. Three of the four most inaccurate years (1958, 1960, 1969, weighted average: 86.3 percent) were years with Republican presidents and Democratic congressional majorities. The coexistence of majority party cue-givers and minority presidents probably confuses cue-taking patterns. The fourth inaccurate year, 1968, like other presidential election years in the period (weighted average for 1960, 1964, and 1968 is 86.7 percent) seems to reflect the disturbing influence of presidential politics on the affairs of the House. The Congress noted by historians for its unusual burst of legislative activity, the Eighty-ninth (1965–1966), is the Congress most accurately simulated (weighted average: 89.3 percent). Perhaps the improved accuracy of these years is due to the fact that, as noted by several members, party cues were stronger during the Eighty-ninth than ever before or since.

ACCURACY BY ROLL CALL

While our model of decision-making in the House usually results in correct predictions, it does make mistakes. An examination of these errors may tell us more about the adequacy of our theory and/or our operationalization of it. Thus the remainder of this chapter is devoted to a careful look at when, and later with whom, LEARN goes wrong.

The Substance of Issues

The subject-matter *content* of a motion shows no relationship to the predictive accuracy of the model. Similarly the issue domain, operationalized as committee of origin, is unrelated to predictive accuracy.[22] Patterns of individual decision-making appear homogeneous across the scope of legislative activity, from farm subsidies to post office construction to "Great Society" issues and defense policy. There are two reasons why this is so, one theoretical, one operational. The theoretical explanantion is the same set of premises that explains cue-taking itself; namely, the compelling need for simplicity of decision-making. That need is better met by a simple (hence homogeneous) decision strategy than one that requires the juggling of response hierarchies from issue to issue.[23]

At the operational level, cue-response patterns are measured across 50 heterogeneous issues, hence for any given member the occurrence of idiosyncratic response by issue could have little effect on his overall (50-vote) cue-response hierarchy. If, for example, a member ordinarily took his cues from his state delegation but looked to the president for cues on foreign policy matters, the foreign policy votes would be just 1 or 2 out of 50 and unlikely to be reflected in the member's response hierarchies. Only if a large number of members followed such a pattern would it be reflected in our measures of accuracy by roll call.

Our operational model, based as it is on the assumption of uniform cue-response patterns across all policy areas, is incapable of a fair test of the notion that cue-taking strategies differ across policy areas. Aage Clausen, for example, begins his analysis of decision-making by congressmen with an assumption of idiosyncratic decision strategies:

> It is the assumption of the policy dimension theory of decision-making . . . that, with rare exception, the decision rule is chosen *after* the policy content has been determined.[24]

Mixed and scattered references in our interview transcripts do not fully support this position or ours, but suggest that both uniform and idiosyncratic strategies are employed by different members. To the extent that our assumption of uniform strategies is incorrect, the accuracy of our operational model is reduced.

The Division of the Vote

The size of winning majorities on a given vote *is* related to predictive accuracy. That relationship is a strong one, but it is not simple. Figure 6-1 displays the means and standard deviations of predictive accuracy at different divisions of the vote. The continuous line of the figure represents mean accuracy, and the vertical lines display standard deviations at each division of the vote.

The near linear relationship between majority size and accuracy in the 75 to 100 percent majority range is predictable. As majorities grow larger and larger prediction gets easier. Cue-givers begin to line up all on one side, reducing the possibilities of conflicting evaluations and the sensitivity of the model to errors in identifying response hierarchies, until in the limiting case of the unanimous vote (there were 125 of them in the 1965–1969 period), it becomes difficult not to predict accurately.

The relationship between majority size and accuracy in the 50 to 75 percent majority range is less predictable. The very closest votes are just below average in predictive accuracy but, as the roll calls become more

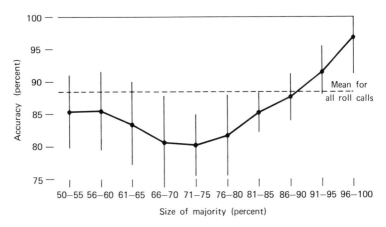

FIGURE 6-1   Accuracy of roll-call predictions by size of majority. Mean and standard deviation. The continuous line is drawn through group means. Vertical lines represent standard deviations.

lopsided, accuracy begins to taper off to a low point in the 66 to 70 percent range. The distribution of accuracy for the whole range of majority sized can be reasonably well represented ($r = .68$) by the parabolic equation:

$$Y = 81.55 + .018 \, (69.34 - x)^2$$

where

Y = percent accurate predictions for roll call;
X = percent in majority for roll call.[25]

The initial constant (81.55) represents the minimum point of the curve. The curve takes on a value of just over 88 percent for 50-50 votes, declines to the minimum as majority size approaches 70 percent, and then rises to 98.5 percent for unanimous votes.

With the close votes predicted at near average accuracy, and the predictive accuracy of the model for extremely lopsided votes easily explainable, the interpretive task at hand is to account for the model's poor performance on some 200 roll calls in the middle of the range. That performance is poor only relatively—at its minimum the accuracy curve is only a little over 6 percent below average overall accuracy, but the differences are still real. The data points are quite consistent, closely fitting the parabola for the whole distribution and particularly so in the middle range.

We note first that majorities in this 66 to 80 percent range are *relatively* infrequent. Accounting for 30 percent of the full range of possible majority sizes, this inaccurate range contains only 20 percent of all roll calls in the period.[26] It is probably true that most roll-call votes are held for one of two reasons: (1) on close issues the roll call is the final House procedure to settle the issue; and (2) on noncontroversial issues roll calls are held because members want their positions on record. Votes in the 66 to 80 percent majority range are neither close enough to require a roll call for the first reason (excepting votes requiring two-thirds majorities; e.g., votes to "suspend the rules") nor so free of controversy to be good candidates for the second reason.

Second, if we presume the basic voting cleavage in the contemporary House to be between non-Southern Demcrats on one side and everybody else on the other, neither side has ever been large enough in recent years to achieve majorities in the 66 to 80 percent range. Thus these middle-range majorities must either be coalitions in which substantial numbers of members cross lines from their normal positions or, alternatively, completely different voting alignments. The latter occurs when the pragmatic congressional "center" votes against a coalition of ideologues from "left" and "right."[27] When "strange bedfellows" combine to produce a majority, the accuracy of our model suffers.

Another factor that may explain some inaccurate predictions in the middle range of majority sizes is that some members sometimes change their voting on an issue when they discover it is not going to be close. Conditional voting commitments ("I'll vote for your side if you need my vote, otherwise I'll vote it the other way") are common on Capitol Hill, although probably not as frequent as newspaper reports of close votes would indicate.[28] Perhaps more common is the behavior of members who switch to their party's position if they know their vote will not alter the outcome of an issue. Their motivation is simple and less then dramatic. If the vote is not particularly important to the member or salient to his district and not close either, to vote the party leadership position may build credit for the future; and to vote against it is a needless irritation.

> . . . . they do keep the feeling behind them, the old Sam Rayburn feeling "that the way to get along is to go along." Unless there is some special reason in your community, your area, your district, why you would desert your leadership on a particular subject, I think they make it clear that they hope and expect you to go along with the leadership. They will forgive you when they know you can't support some issue, but in return they expect you to go along on these issues that don't make too much difference one way or the other.

Southern Democrats, with their typically bad party records, may be particularly inclined to switch to party support on these nonsalient and not-close votes to repair their standing with the Democratic leaders.

The Parliamentary Situation

Table 6-2 demonstrates some substantial differences in mean accuracy of prediction by the *type of motion* being voted upon. Two of the more common types of votes, final passage and conference report motions, are predicted more accurately than average; all others average or less. But the type of motion under consideration is also related to majority sizes. The distribution of final passage votes, for example, is heavily skewed toward the unanimous end of the scale. Noncontroversial legislation is seldom the subject of roll-call votes on rules, amendments, or motions to recommit; one public vote on final passage suffices to be recorded in staunch support of motherhood and apple pie.

In Table 6-3, the various types of votes (regrouped to increase cell sizes) are reexamined, controlling for majority size. Cell entries are percentage point deviations from average predictive accuracy for each group of majority sizes. The small—and in every case in-

TABLE 6-2   ACCURACY BY PARLIAMENTARY SITUATION

Type	Number of Votes	Percent Accurate	Deviation from Mean Accuracy[a]
Final passage	468	90.7	+2.5
Conference report	113	88.7	+0.5
Rule	50	88.2	0
Recommit with instructions	125	86.4	−1.8
Suspend rules	26	85.9	−2.3
Procedural motion and other	90	85.8	−2.4
Resolution	47	85.4	−2.8
Amendment	91	85.2	−3.0
Simple recommit	39	81.5	−6.7
Total	1049		

[a] Mean accuracy = 88.2 percent.

consistent—deviations from average predictive accuracy clearly indicate that overall deviations from average accuracy are very largely a function of the size of majorities that typically accompany the various parliamentary situations.[29]

Early Votes: The Learning Curve

Early-in-the-session votes are less accurately predicted than others for a variety of reasons. The first is that the memory of the simulator starts with the beginning of the session. With a very small sample of votes from which to measure cue-response patterns we would expect some unreliability in the inference of cue hierarchies. More precisely, we would expect that:

1.   Accuracy would start low and gradually rise until it reached the average level.

2.   The accuracy of early predictions would fluctuate due to the

TABLE 6-3   DEVIATIONS FROM AVERAGE PREDICTIVE ACCURACY BY
PARLIAMENTARY SITUATION, GROUPED ON MAJORITY
SIZE

		Majority Size			
Procedure	N	50–65%	66–80%	81–95%	96–100%
Final passage	468	−1.2	−0.3	+0.7	−0.1
Recommit with instructions	125	+1.9	+2.9	−3.6	+2.7[a]
Conference report	113	−0.7	+0.3	+0.6	+1.1
Amendment	91	+0.5	−2.4	+0.1	+1.5
Procedural motion	90	0	+3.6	−1.3	−6.5
Other	162	−2.9	−2.1	−1.2	+1.2
Mean accuracy		85.0%	81.3%	88.9%	97.3%
	(N = 1049)	(n = 363)	(n = 212)	(n = 193)	(n = 281)

[a] Only one case.

enhanced influence of single votes in determining cue-response hierarchies.

Figure 6-2 portrays average predictive accuracy by roll-call number[30] for the five years simulated by the LEARN program. A linear regression of accuracy over roll-call number for the first 22 roll calls shows that the data largely conform to expectations. Accuracy does indeed start out at a low point (79.6 percent) and rise (slope = +.33) to average. A glance at the scatter plot also indicates that the expected fluctuation of accuracy of early predictions also occurs, leading to a relatively low correlation of +.17.

One expectation is not met. If adding information adds reliability to cue-response measurement we would not expect a linear relationship, but instead a curve with a negative second derivative. That is, we would expect a dramatic improvement in reliability (and therefore accuracy) by the addition of one roll call at the begining (reflected in a high positive slope in the accuracy curve) when information is scantiest, but only a marginal improvement (low positive slope) and eventually no improvement (zero slope) as more and more votes have contributed to the measurement of response patterns. Such a pattern does not appear. Probably the principal reason that the curve is "straightened out" is that the very earliest votes are sometimes accurately predicted because they are party-line votes, particularly in the odd numbered years where they may be votes on the organization of the House. The simulator quickly develops a party-line mentality under these circumstances, and may do exceedingly well if a series of

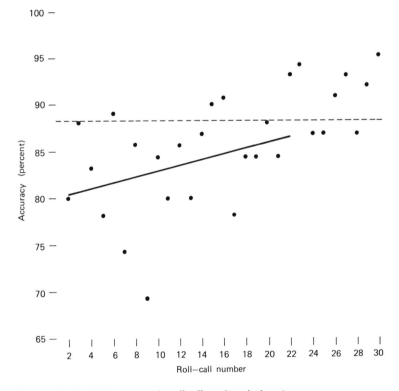

FIGURE 6-2   Predictive accuracy by roll-call number: the learning curve.

early votes all break on party lines. Removing these party votes from the analysis would result in both lower initial accuracy and a nonlinear improvement.

Theory Testing and Predictive Accuracy: "Core Votes"

To this point we have not discriminated between roll calls as tests of the cue-taking model. We have predicted everything and treated every roll call as an equal test of the model. We have resisted the notion that somehow one set of roll calls could be isolated that were in some way more "significant" or more "typical" than others. But clearly some votes are better tests of our theory and operational model than others—even if not necessarily "typical." In some cases the model should predict well even if the theory is wrong, in others the theory itself predicts that accuracy of the model should be low.

Votes that pass with lopsided majorities are not good tests of theory both because they lack the controvesy over public policy that interests students of law-making bodies and because some of them are too easily predicted to reflect well on any theory. Thus in an attempt to get at a "core" of votes that should be good tests of the theory we eliminate all votes where the winning side had 66 percent of the votes or more. What remains are closely contested votes.

If the model's predictive accuracy on lopsided votes does not lend much credence to the theory, neither does the inaccuracy of early-in-the-session votes detract from it. That inaccuracy is clearly a function not of the theory of cue-taking, but of the peculiarities of the operational model.[31] Thus we delete the first 22 roll calls of each session from our sample of core votes, again not because they are in any way atypical, but because they are not good tests of the theory.

Predictive accuracy for the remaining "core" votes (320 in the five-year period) is 85.2 percent, a drop of 2.9 percentage points from overall accuracy.[32] What are we to make of that? We noted earlier that judgments of accuracy are largely a function of expectations. With a sample of this size, 51 percent accuracy is a statistically significant improvement over chance, but clearly everyone would regard it a dramatic failure. How high must accuracy be to be successful? What are the expectations for the predictive accuracy of what we have called "core" votes? Certainly they are lower than for all votes, but it is not clear how much. The predictive capability of simple prediction rules (e.g., all members vote Yea, or all members vote with the majority) is drastically reduced when only closely contested votes are examined. If they establish the context of expectations, then 85.2 percent on "core" votes is quite a dramatic showing—more so than the original 88.1 percent accuracy for all votes. In any case, it is clear that the model does *not* depend on large numbers of uncontested votes for a substantial proportion of its predictive accuracy.

ACCURACY BY MEMBER

Our model thus accurately predicts the votes of House members on a wide variety of roll calls. But does it systematically bomb-out in predicting the voting decisions of any identifiable subgroups of members within the chamber?

The votes of our hundred-member interview sample were simulated along with all other members and, since we know a good deal about these members, we shall use them as the sample for this analysis. The price paid for the richness of interview data is, of course, that this analysis is thereby limited to a sample of 100 members for only one year, 1969. But this seems a price worth paying.

The bar graph of Figure 6-3 portrays the distribution of individual member accuracy scores for 1969. The year was not one of the simulator's better ones, and average accuracy for the interview sample (85.9 percent) was a little lower than that of the whole House (86.7 percent). That difference is within the realm of sampling fluctuation, and could largely be eliminated by the deletion of the one member at the extreme left of the figure—by far the greatest predictive failure in the entire House that year.

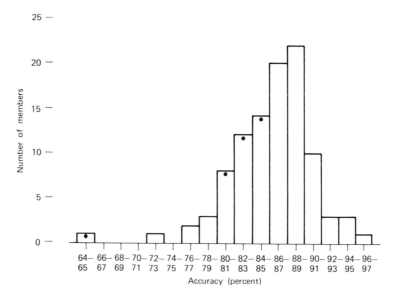

Figure 6-3 Predictive accuracy by member, 1969. Asterisked columns include members who say that they do not take cues.

Members Who Do Not Take Cues

Four members we interviewed were classified as non-cue-takers, two because they explicitly said so, and two others because they fostered the impression by refusing to discuss the matter.[33] All were simulated with less than average accuracy, although some not much so. As a group they were 8 percent below average accuracy.

One member, a veteran Midwestern Republican, provides a striking demonstration that a model predicated upon cue-taking is not much good at predicting the behavior of a genuine non-cue-taker. We accurately predicted his votes only 64 percent of the time in 1969, an unimpressive showing by any standard.

We have frequently quoted member explanantions of cue-taking in previous chapters. The remarks of this member round out the picture somewhat. They are a consistent statement of a counterview. On specialization, he says:

> I don't know. I change off. It's hard for me to point out one area; I'm in-
> volved in almost everything that comes down the line. . . .
> I'll know something about every bill that comes to the floor—and this
> is true of the bills on the Private Consent Calendars. . . . Well they all
> have to be read if you want to know anything about them—each one
> separately. You can't know everything there is to know about a bill, but
> you can know about every bill that comes in, see?

On the allocation of his time:

> I know something about everything that comes to the House floor. I may
> not know all there is to know about them. . . . Obviously you have to give
> quite a bit of time to legislation if you're going to know something about
> every bill that comes along. . . .

On low-information decision-making:

> On there are a good many members of Congress who pay no attention or
> very little attention to bills that have no direct effect on their district [or]
> their states.

On the committees:

> Why are so few members to be found on the House floor when there is
> business being transacted? . . . It isn't conducive to the best legislation
> when they're not there. Because they can't know. . . . Much as I may try
> to keep up with the oncoming bills, I still profit from the debate on the
> House floor. I just feel this is true of most of the rest of them. Sure the
> committee knows, *but that is not enough.*

In short, he paints an uncommon picture of a man who, with some
considerable frustration, tries to inform himself on every bill. It is a
picture that accords well with his reputation in the House. A member
from the same state says:

> Many times when I've gone over to the floor to vote . . . somebody comes
> in and says, "What's the vote on this issue?" or "What's up?" I know it

happens quite frequently. In my own case I've been a little more sensitive about this, because [he] took me by the hand when I first came to Congress and he said, "You'd better damn well know what's going on!" And in the early days here, If I didn't I got scolded pretty thoroughly by him, because he knows more of what's going on here than any other member of the House.

Another of the four non-cue-takers is a more marginal classification. He is a self-proclaimed specialist, and yet he also claims across-the-board knowledge of legislation:

> Of course the only thing that's available to me is the committee report on every bill. And I wouldn't cast a vote unless I read the report, unless I knew something about the bill . . . I would never vote on a bill that I didn't know something about.

He is one of that small band of inveterate attenders of debate in the Committee of the Whole. Like the first member, he says he pays special attention to private bills. This would seem to make him a non-cue-taker. But his votes are not particularly difficult to predict. Our model predicts his voting at only 1 percent below average accuracy for the five-year period. Even though this member is evidently better informed outside his specialty than most, he may still take cues from those better informed than he on many issues. As a specialist, unlike the first member, he is probably more aware of the limitations of the nonspecialist, and hence more likely to defer to the judgment of others.

Two other non-cue-takers are much alike.[34] Both are senior members of the Rules Committee. To a very great extent membership on Rules is a functional alternative to cue-taking. Members of the committee are in a uniquely fortunate position to inform themselves on major issues.[35] Committee hearings focus on the central arguments and feature the central actors. Staff work is directed heavily toward improving member information. Contact with party leadership is frequent. And, not least important, committee members have no substantive interest to distract their attention.[36]

Both of our committee members are from districts that are "safe"

by any definition, hence both have far more time to devote to legislative duties than does the typical member. Their frequent interaction
on a formal basis with the actors we have called initial cue-givers
largely obviates the need for informal cue-taking. These two members
are less accurately predicted than average, 3 percent and 5 percent
respectively, but not dramatically so.

Our four non-cue-takers illustrate the kinds of factors that make
cue-taking the *normal*, but not the *only* mode of decision in the House.
Two members have assigned themselves the task of keeping close watch
on the small, routine, and largely private legislation. That task is almost a specialty in itself, and they defer to no one in it. The other two
have as their committee specialty the surveillance of most major legislation. Although they are regularly in a position to communicate with important cue-givers, they also bring to their decisions information
resources beyond the reach of most members. All four operate something like textbook congressmen.

The Other Ninety-Six Percent

For the 96 members who said they sometimes made decisions by cue-
taking there is relatively little variation in accuracy of prediction—and
hence relatively little variation to explain.[37] Very little of what we
know about these members is related to accurate or inaccurate prediction. The relationships that do appear are mostly weak and not statistically significant. If our measurement were better and the sample
larger, most, we suspect, would still remain unimpressive. Thus the
following discussion illustrates the limits of our understanding of the
factors that explain variations in the predictive accuracy of our model.
We turn first to group level variations.

GROUP DIFFERENCES IN ACCURACY. Our model has consistently
predicted the votes of Democrats a little better than Republicans. For
our interview sample in 1969 that difference remains, but is reduced
considerably (Table 6-4), perhaps due to the omission of the four non-

TABLE 6-4   MEAN ACCURACY OF PREDICTION BY PARTY (PERCENT)

Party	Entire Sample	96 Cue-Takers
Democrats	86.8 (n = 50)	86.9 (n = 49)
Republicans	85.1 (n = 50)	85.6 (n = 47)
Difference	1.7[a] (N = 100)	1.3[b] (N = 96)

[a] Significance: p < .05 (one tailed).
[b] Significance: p < .10 (one tailed).

cue-takers (three of whom were Republicans) and probably in part due to the divided control of the White House and Congress in 1969.

Partisan differences in predictive accuracy appear to be largely a function of membership in partisan subgroups rather than in the legislative party as such. Table 6-5 breaks down mean accuracy scores by membership in sociolegislative groups within the parties. A modest, but statistically significant difference appears between the predictive accuracy average for Democratic Study Group members and Republican sociolegislative group members. More important, there is virtually no difference in mean accuracy for the two parties when group members are excluded.

TABLE 6-5   MEAN   ACCURACY   OF   PREDICTION,   BY   PARTY   AND
            SOCIOLEGISLATIVE GROUP MEMBERSHIP (PERCENT)

	Group Members[a]	Nonmembers
Democrats	87.2 (n = 31)	86.4 (n = 19)
Republicans	85.0 (n = 19)	86.0 (n = 31)
Difference	2.2[b] (N = 50)	0.4 (N = 50)

[a] The group membership for all sample Democrats is the Democratic Study Group; sample Republicans belong to a variety of small discussion groups.
[b] Significance: p < .05 (one-tailed).

Like the sociolegislative groups, party delegations from each state might contribute to interparty differences if delegation effects occur. If delegations act as decision-making units rather than just collections of members sharing common attributes, we might expect some systematic deviations in predictive accuracy from both the means for the House and for the parties. If no delegation effects occurred—that is, if each delegation were something like a random sample of House members—then we would expect delegation accuracy means to be very closely bunched around the mean for the House, except in the smaller delegations where some large deviations could occur by chance. We have examined the 18 largest delegations with a view toward isolating systematic variations that might be attributed to delegation effects.[38] Table 6-6 shows 9 delegations to deviate significantly from the House mean.

TABLE 6-6 MEAN ACCURACY OF PREDICTION, BY STATE PARTY DELEGATIONS, 1969

Delegation	Mean Accuracy (percent)	Deviation from House Mean (percent)	
Pennsylvania Democrats	92.2	+5.5	$p < .001$[a]
Massachusetts Democrats	91.7	+5.0	$p < .01$
New Jersey Democrats	91.1	+4.4	$p < .01$
Indiana Democrats	91.1	+4.4	$p < .025$
Michigan Democrats	91.1	+4.4	$p < .025$
Illinois Democrats	89.2	+2.5	$p < .05$
House Mean	86.7	—	—
Illinois Republicans	84.2	−2.5	$p < .05$
Pennsylvania Republicans	83.3	−3.4	$p < .01$
Ohio Republicans	82.8	−3.9	$p < .001$

[a] Probability of obtaining the observed deviation from sampling fluctuation alone, one-tailed.

All Democratic delegations were above the mean for the House and all Republicans below it. Nor can these differences be explained away by partisanship. If delegation means are compared to party means (instead of the mean for the whole House) only three deviations become nonsignificant; they are for the Illinois and Pennsylvania Republicans and the Illinois Democrats.

Treating the Ohio Republicans as something of a fluke—they are the only large delegation significantly below their party average—it appears that *strong* delegation effects are to be found only in the Democratic Party. When differences are statistically significant (5 of 9 cases), predictive accuracy is uniformly higher for the delegations than for the party as a whole. Thus, another part of apparent interparty differences in accuracy may be explained without reference to the legislative party itself.

INDIVIDUAL ATTRIBUTES.   There are few individual attributes related to predictive accuracy. Seniority, the all-purpose variable of legislative research, is completely uncorrelated ($r = 0.000$) with predictive accuracy, for example. We have seen that party is only weakly related to it.

Variables that do seem to be related to predictive accuracy relate to

TABLE 6-7   MEAN ACCURACY OF PREDICTION BY 1968 MARGIN OF VICTORY[a]

Margin	Mean Accuracy (percent)	N
Close (less than 55 percent)	87.6	21
Medium (56–67 percent)	86.3	38
Safe (more than 67 percent)	85.4	37

[a] Mean predictive accuracy for 96 cue-takers = 86.25 percent. Product moment correlation between victory percentage and predictive accuracy = −.18.

TABLE 6-8 MEAN ACCURACY OF PREDICTION BY NUMBER OF LEGISLATIVE SPECIALTIES

Number of Specialties Mentioned	Mean Accuracy (percent)	N
1	87.6	22
2	86.5	41
3 or more	85.1	33
		96

Product moment correlation $= -.21$.

how members apportion their time. The model seems to predict the voting of members with heavy nonlegislative work loads better than that of members with more time to devote to their strictly legislative duties. We have been forced to measure this quite indirectly by examining the margin of victory each member received in the previous election and inferring that the smaller the margin of victory for each member the greater the proportion of his time he will spend on activities related to getting reelected and the less on strictly legislative duties.[39] This is, of course, a very arguable inference. The best we can say in its defense is that it seems a reasonable interpretation and others we have considered do not. We have examined a number of "third variables" that are correlated with victory margin (e.g., seniority and perceived electoral security), but all of them fail to be correlated with accuracy and hence do not seem to explain the relationship between victory margin and predictive accuracy.

We are better able to assess the effects of specialty-related behavior on predictive accuracy. We have two measures of the "focus" of specialization for each member. One is simply the number of distinct specialties, as volunteered by the member (Table 6-8), and the other is the degree of overlap between specialties and formal committee assignments (Table 6-9). Both are weakly related to predictive accuracy. Both indicate that the more concentrated and single-minded the

TABLE 6-9   MEAN ACCURACY OF PREDICTION BY RELATIONSHIP OF SPECIALTIES AND COMMITTEE ASSIGNMENTS

Member Specializes Exclusively in Areas of Committee Work	Mean Accuracy (percent)	N
Yes	87.0	48
No	85.5	48
		96

member the more likely we are to predict accurately. For the less focused and concentrated congressmen, fewer decisions need to be made by cue-taking.

Predictive accuracy is a strange attribute to associate with members. It is not descriptive of their behavior in any direct fashion but rather is a summary of the fit of their behavior to a specific operational model. If the votes of individual members are inaccurately predicted, it may be that they do not take cues, or that they take cues in a different way from the specific model imposed on them, or that they take cues with less frequency than other members. It may be a mixture of all three. With accuracy scores difficult to interpret and tightly clustered around a central tendency as we have found them to be, it is not surprising that few attributes successfully discriminate between the easy predictions and the hard ones. The picture that emerges is of relatively undifferentiated behavior in roll-call decision-making.

CONCLUSIONS

Computer simulation is fashionable these days. But although it has many strengths as a research tool, simulation does not provide the ultimate and definitive test of theory that we would like. All a simulation can do is increase (if it is successful) or decrease (if it fails) one's confidence in the theory upon which it is based.

Our simulation, predicated on the view that members of the House of Representatives normally cast their roll-call votes on the basis of cues from their colleagues, successfully predicts the behavior of members by following a process we believe to be analogous to that followed by "real" congressmen. Members of the House, 96 of the 100 we interviewed, say they vote by taking cues with considerable frequency. These two independent and very different tests of our theory thus point to the same conclusion: members vote by taking cues.

So what? We look at this question in the next, and final, chapter of this book.

NOTES

1. A technical description of the simulation programs can be found in Appendix C.

2. See our discussion of deviant cases in Chapter 3.

3. For a more extended and more specific discussion of the role of computer simulations in this research, see James A. Stimson, "The Diffusion of Evaluations: Patterns of Cue-Taking in the United States House of Representatives," Unpublished Doctoral Dissertation, University of North Carolina, 1970, Chapter I.

4. Note the implicit assumption that nonvoting is irrelevant to cue-taking and therefore unpredictable. Genuine abstention we believe is rare in the United States Congress; most nonvoting is due to member absences, not refusal to take positions. Recall from Chapter 3 the political hazards of missing votes.

5. That the assertion of the descriptive accuracy of the simulation was untestable was the major reason for the congressional interviewing program.

6. Several readers of our early work have suggested that we follow the practice of the Weather Service and make probabilistic predictions of the form, "Member i has an $x\%$ chance of voting 'Yea' on roll call j." That is consistent with the theory of cue-taking and easy to do. We choose not to do it because: (1) it diminishes the analogy between model and congressman (albeit, only slightly), and (2) it obscures interpretation of results.

7. Number 7 is a partial exception; the simulation results do provide some evidence for it individually.

8. The most important cue sources that are missing from the simulations, to judge from the interviews, are rank-and-file committee members. They could not have been included without building in, at the same time, a high probability of many spuriously accurate predictions. Their influence is felt however in the various intermediary cue-givers, where they are an early and crucial part of the nuclei of majority sentiments.

9.   We are indebted to W. Phillips Shively and Duncan MacRae, Jr., for detailed and insightful critiques of our early work, which were particularly helpful on the question of spurious accuracy.

10. The chief sources of voting cues mentioned in the interviews, but not considered in the simulation design are the Republican sociolegislative groups, whose influence we did not appreciate. They have however been noted in the literature. See Charles L. Clapp, *The Congressman: His Work As He Sees It* (Washington: The Brookings Institution, 1963), Chapter 1, "The Member and His Colleagues."

11. Specifically excluded is empirical determination of parameters, allowing the computer to optimize prediction by systematic variation of parameters. While empirical determination makes sense in some contexts, here the number of predictions and their complexity encouraged us to pay the price of a loss of predictive accuracy (probably a small one) in order to have an intuitively justifiable operational model. See Stimson, *op. cit.*, Chapter 1, for a more extended discussion of this point.

12. Compiled and copyrighted by Congressional Quarterly, Inc., Washington, D.C. The annual volumes from 1957 through 1969 have been utilized.

13. The Speaker of the House cannot be used as an operational cue-giver, because he does not vote. However well his position may be known to members of his party, it can't feasibly be determined for the operational model.

14. See D. R. Matthews and J. A. Stimson, "Decision-Making by U.S. Representatives: A Preliminary Model," in S. Sidney Ulmer (ed.), *Political Decision-Making* (New York: Van Nostrand-Reinhold, 1970) for an earlier definition and discussion.

15. The nuisance exceptions are party leaders (4 members) and DSG leaders (7 members), who are likely to take cues from themselves on those votes where their respective cues are available. Their nuisance value is that they would be easy to predict in any case—without circularity. The circularity could have been eliminated with special routines for these 11 members, but the difference in percentage (total) accuracy would have been so small (probably no more than 0.01 percent) as to not justify the special attention. The possibility of circularity exists for committee chairmen and ranking minority members, but is considerably less likely to have any effect—certainly no appreciable effect—than party and DSG leaders. The reason is that the chairman's own position could only serve as a cue to him if: (1) his committee reported the bill, *and* (2) the chairman (role) was his highest cue-giver, very infrequently the case. Similar logic applies to ranking minority members.

16. Matthews and Stimson, *op. cit.*, describes the first model, SIMULATE, and contains a proposal for the second, INDCUE. INDCUE and a third program, CUETEST, were measurement programs whose output was input for SIMULATE, which did the actual simulation. The LEARN program described above combines the measurement and prediction aspects of the simulation.

17. The actual sequence of the three functions in LEARN is different than we present them here, but for purely technical reasons. The logic is identical.

18. On the first roll call of the session the measurement segment is bypassed and arbit-

rary information (every member votes with party majority) passed on to the pre-diction segment. That produces 100 percent accuracy on votes for Speaker in the first session of a Congress and mixed results on the first vote of the second session.

19. Note that .500 is only an approximation of expected chance agreement, perfectly accurate only in the limiting case of a 50-50 split. Assuming a 65-35 percentage split to be closer to average, the proportion of chance agreements between two members is equal to the probability that the cue-giver is in the majority (.65) times the probability that the cue-taker is in the majority (.65) plus the probability that the cue-giver is in the minority (.35) times the probability that the cue-taker is in the minority (.35) or $(.65 \times .65 = .4225) + (.35 \times .35 = .1225) = .545$. We use .500 for its intuitive appeal, because adjusting the parameter for the average size of the majority on the last 50 votes after each roll call is burdensome and adds complexity to a model already too complex, and because we fear it might spu-riously inflate the importance of negative cue-taking to use a higher figure. The model already contains a tie-breaking device that (unintentionally) resolves ties between positive and negative cue-scores in favor of the negative, with some strange results in early-in-the-session votes.

20. This is a simpler procedure for prediction than in the earlier models. They treated cue-scores as measures of intensity of predisposition, and combined cue responses (from as many as 3 cue-givers) until "information sufficiency" was reached. In-tellectually appealing, the intensity and information sufficiency notions produced predictions of about the same overall accuracy as the present "one-cue" model, and were abandoned in the interest of parsimony. The interview materials give the impression that members differ in regard to the number of cues they consider suffi-cient for a decision.

21. Casual observations of the massive simulation printouts lead us to believe that the response patterns rarely change within a session and not frequently between sessions, except in the obvious cases where cue-givers change (e.g., Nixon replaces Johnson as President).

22. Where differences do appear between committees, they are explainable by other content free factors such as size of majority.

23. We remind the reader that although cue-giving roles are constant, the individuals filling them (e.g., committee chairmen) may vary from issue to issue.

24. Aage R. Clausen, *How Congressmen Decide: A Policy Focus* (New York: St. Martin, 1973), p. 13. Italics in original.

25. The type of curve (parabola) was chosen from inspection of data points. The focus and two coefficients are the product of a least-squares solution of three si-multaneous equations. M. Ezekiel and K. Fox, *Methods of Correlation and Regression Analysis* (New York: Wiley, 1959).

26. If the *number* of roll calls for all sizes of majorities is examined, the distribution roughly fits a parabola not much dissimilar in shape than the accuracy curve—high at both ends of the range and low in the middle.

27. Only during the Eighty-ninth Congress did either side of the basic voting cleavage

deviate markedly from 50 percent. There, interestingly enough, we find that the inflection point of our accuracy curve shifts to the right slightly (meaning that minimum accuracy occurs with larger than normal majority sizes). This lends some support to the hypothesis that votes in this range are inaccurately predicted because they do not reflect the normal voting cleavage.

28.   In this and most other matters concerning Congress, newspaper accounts seize upon the unusual—because it is newsworthy—so often that it comes to seem usual. Those who "see" Congress through the newspapers see Congress and its members at their most newsworthy, hence abnormal occasions. Many Capitol Hill reporters are insightful observers of Congress, but the newsworthiness criterion guarantees the result of their reporting will be a distorted composite of congressional reality.

29.   Examination of the accuracy residuals (produced by subtracting the effects of the majority-size parabola), shows the same result. No procedural type deviates significantly from its norm predicted by majority size.

30.   Roll calls are numbered chronologically by the date and time they were called. Roll-call number 1 is deleted from the analysis since its predictive accuracy is entirely a function of the arbitrary parameters used to "start off" the simulation. Each data point represents five predictions, one for each year.

31.   In the CUETEST-SIMULATE routine the first session of a Congress was used for measurement of cue-response patterns, and votes were predicted only in the second session. The predictive accuracy for early votes did not diverge from the norm for the whole session. See Matthews and Stimson, *op. cit.* for a fuller description at the CUETEST-SIMULATE routine.

32.   Note that an incidental effect of examining only close votes is the elimination of one cue-giver, "the House Majority" and the probable reduction in the frequency of operationally defined cues from other majoritarian cue sources. Note also that our analysis of "core" votes is *post hoc*; we did not rerun the simulation on the smaller sample of votes, but simply recorded the accuracy obtained on these votes from the original runs. The import of the distinction is that the memory used to predict close votes was a 50-vote sample of *all* votes, not just close ones. If the memory contained only close votes it would probably have done better predicting close votes.

33.   Members were classified as cue-takers or non-cue-takers on the basis of their responses to questions about the frequency of low-information voting and their response to low-information situations (see Appendix A, Questions 10 and 11).

34.   One unfortunate respect in which they were alike is refusal to allow taping of the interviews—hence no quotations.

35.   For legislation exempted from Rules Committee purview see Froman, *The Congressional Process* (New York: Little, Brown, 1967), Chapter 3.

36.   Average accuracy for the three members of the Rules Committee in our sample is 83.7 percent, three points below the norm for the House.

37.   The distribution of accuracy scores in Figure 6-3 is quite a good approximation of a normal curve for a small sample. This has theoretical import. It lends weight to

the hypothesis that *there are few systematic differences between members with regard to accuracy of prediction.* The distribution of accuracy scores presented in Figure 6-3 may be the result of relatively minor fluctuations around a uniform norm for all members. An unhappy implication of the distribution is that even if this hypothesis is wrong, it will be difficult to find much conclusive evidence to the contrary. There is so little variation to explain that significant relationships are elusive. Fifty-two percent of all members are within ±3 percent of the mean. Eighty-six percent lie within ±6 percent. Thus the magnitude of differences to be expected between various subgroups of members is small.

38. Data here are scores for all members of the delegations, not just members interviewed. The 18 delegations account for 233 members or about 54 percent of all members of the House.

39. Our attempts to measure time allocations more directly did not produce satisfactory data. See Appendix A, Questions 7 and 7a.

CHAPTER SEVEN

CONCLUSIONS AND IMPLICATIONS

A legalistic heritage and a democratic ideology have predisposed
American political science to search outside the Washington community
for explanations of behavior in that community—legalism looking to the
Constitution as a determinative influence, and democratic ideology
looking to public opinion and constituency "pressures" as determinative
influences upon the conduct of men in office. . . . Political science has yet
to confront squarely the proposition that the governing group in
Washington . . . has an inner life of its own—a special culture which
carries with it prescriptions and cues for behavior that may be far more
explicit than those originating outside the group, and no less
consequential for the conduct of government.

James S. Young, *The Washington
Community, 1800–1829* (1966).

In this book we have developed and presented a theory of decision-
making by members of the U.S. House of Representatives. Simply put,
the theory is that the normal roll-call votes by members of the lower
house of Congress are cast on the basis of cues obtained from their

legislative colleagues. This hypothesis has been subject to two independent tests: computer simulations and a program of interviews with a sample of House members. Both support the validity of the view that such cues are a major determinant of the votes cast on the House floor. Normally, policy decisions made by a relative handful of members are informally diffused, in ways that we have sought to describe and explain, to the entire membership, who in turn adopt these evaluations as their own. By casting their Yeas and Nays ,the members transform these cues into authoritative decisions of the House of Representatives.

In this chapter we comment briefly upon some implications of this finding, sometimes in a quite speculative way.

LIMITATIONS OF THE CUE-TAKING THEORY

Our theory, stated above within the context of the House of Representatives, is really quite general. With suitable assumptions about decision constraints, it can be derived as a special case of Simon's "behavioral model of rational choice,"[1] a model intended to apply to a wide range of decision-making. If our concern, however, is in understanding *legislatures* in general (rather than *decision-making* in general) much important activity is excluded from its predictive and explanatory purview.

The theory of cue-taking focuses on the *final* decision processes leading to the enactment of public policy. We believe this to be a more promising research strategy than studying presumed causal factors more removed from the immediate output of political activity. Once these final processes are understood, we can work backwards in what Campbell and his associates[2] call the "funnel of causality" toward the ultimate causes of legislative decisions.

But this means that cue-taking theory, by itself, does not provide adequate answers to questions about phenomena occurring *early* in the legislative process or *early* in the careers of legislators.

The Origins of Cues

We have only tenuously suggested explanations for the origins of cues. Cues are defined by those who choose to follow them. We have found that members with certain personal attributes who occupy specific formal positions in the House are more likely to be chosen as cue-givers than others. We have also found that different types of members have different propensities to follow different cue sources. But the development of member decision strategies, the decisions on how to make decisions, remains unexplored.

For example, all cue-takers in the House face the choice of following either what we have called initial cue-givers or intermediaries. The initial cue-givers are laden with expertise, and often legitimacy as well; the intermediaries are frequently reference groups, sources of ideological and partisan consistency. The cue-taker's choice between initial and intermediary cue-givers might be characterized as between unquestionable expertise based on questionable value premises on the one hand, and questionable expertise based on unquestionable value premises on the other. Whether the empirical or the value premises are to be given greater weight is a question on which reasonable men of different temperament can disagree. The choice members make may reflect such psychological traits as inner/other directedness, ego strength, and the like. It may also have to do with career aspirations—members pursuing a career in the House may look to very different sorts of cue-givers than those whose ambitions lie elsewhere. But this is speculative; research remains to be done on the development of cue-taking strategies. What seems reasonably clear, in any case, is that these decision strategies evolve during the members' apprentice years in the House, or even earlier, and have a lasting impact on the pattern of member votes.

The Early Stages of the Legislative Process

Our theory also fails to shed much light on decisions made during the early stages of the legislative process. This is not an altogether unhappy state of affairs, for it is precisely these early decisions that are best treated by the now voluminous literature on legislatures and legislative behavior. The application of well-developed social theories to the decision-making of small groups—especially legislative committees—is the outstanding achievement of research on Congress during the past decade.[3] But these studies ordinarily have not been able to explain later decisions on the floor. Our approach, of course, has just the opposite problem.

The two types of studies, focusing on two qualitatively different stages in the legislative process, are complementary. The output of committees, subcommittees, policy-subsystems, and other aspects of the legislative process that have been much studied is a set of cues for the larger congressional system: the required input for the cue-taking decision model. The analyst of the early stages of the legislative process cannot explain the ultimate influence of cues within his theory; we cannot explain their origin within ours. Together the two approaches may come close to explaining the entire legislative process.

CUE-TAKING AND PUBLIC POLICY

Cue-taking is a shortcut way of making reasonable decisions, but how good a shortcut is it?

We have asserted that cue-taking produces for the member a decision similar to that he would have arrived at had he undertaken individual and independent analysis and evaluation. If the results were always the same by either process, the net effect of cue-taking on public policy would be zero. If the results of the two methods differed only by infrequent and random fluctuations, the net effect would approach zero. Only if the results of decisions reached by cue-taking regularly and systematically differ from those derived through independent evaluation do the processes described in this book have much effect on public policy.

Such systematic and regular divergence might come about in either of two ways. First, starting with a group of initial cue-givers with views representative of the attitudes of the House, the process by which cues are diffused might so emphasize some cues at the expense of others that the final collective decision would be unrepresentative. Or second, starting with an unrepresentative set of initial cue-givers, the diffusion process might accurately reflect their unrepresentative positions, thus also resulting in an unrepresentative collective decision. Of course a decision that is unrepresentative of House opinions is not necessarily unrepresentative of the electorate. But that is a large and complex question that we must leave to other researchers to explore.[4] The question that concerns us here is whether or not the cue-giving and cue-taking process itself has a significant policy bias.

The first logically possible source of policy bias in the cue-diffusion process does not seem likely. As we have seen, the process of diffusion is complex, and cue-takers are ordinarily confronted with multiple and conflicting policy evaluations from which to choose. Partisan and ideological antagonisms between intermediaries are common. This would seem to guarantee that any conflicts of evaluation among initial cue-givers will be mirrored, and probably even intensified, in the diffusion process.

The second possible source of policy bias in the cue-diffusion process, unrepresentative initial cue-givers, is more troublesome. Members of the contemporary House tend to place a high value on expertise in their choice of cue-givers. Which members of the House are perceived as experts on various subjects depends partly on their choice of specialty area. And most congressmen—82 percent of all those members we interviewed who considered themselves specialist—tend to specialize in subjects of particular interest to their constituents (Table 7-1). Impressive numbers also mention personal reasons—their previous training and occupation, for example—for deciding to devote the bulk of their time and energy to a legislative specialty. Still others, particularly those tilling the least interesting vineyards of government, report developing a legislative interest only after serving on a committee to which they had not asked to be assigned. But to the extent that the development of expertise is a matter of personal choice, the experts on a given subject are *not* likely to be a representative sample of the membership of the House. Rather,

TABLE 7-1   REASONS FOR SPECIALTY

Reasons	Number of Mentions	Percent of Specialists	Percent of All Mentions
Personal history			
Education and training	13	13	6
Previous occupation	21	22	10
Personal experience and background	42	43	19
Service in other legislature	15	15	7
Political factors			
Constituency relevance	80	82	36
Other factors			
Committee responsibilities[a]	47	48	21
Service in the House	3	3	1
Total	221	[b]	100

[a] The "committee responsibilities" category is coded as a reason only when substantial interest in the policy area resulted from an unrequested committee assignment.

[b] Respondents were allowed to give up to three reasons, and many did, hence the sum of the percentages of respondents giving each reasons is greater than 100 percent.

they usually possess especially compelling motivations of a personal or political sort for their choice of specialty.

This phenomenon has been often noted as far as membership on legislative *committees* is concerned. But unrepresentative committees do not inevitably result in unrepresentative policy decisions on the floor. Cues emanating from committee members need not prevail over other sources of policy information and evaluation. But if all the initial cue-givers in a policy domain—be they members of the relevant committee or not—tend to be a biased sample of the House, the probability of unrepresentative policy decisions is very substantial. As long as expertise remains a major basis for the acceptance of cues, the policy decisions of the House are likely to be biased in favor of those groups and individuals most directly and immediately affected by these decisions.

A HOUSE WITHOUT WINDOWS?[5]

To watch Congress at work is to be impressed by the truth of Young's assertion of an inner life in the Washington community. The inner life is a necessity for few outside of the community are interested in the pressing details of the daily operation of a national government. The community is built around a shared knowledge of legislative life—not least of the legislation itself—which is neither interesting nor important to the public at large. The community is open to anyone who will acquire the requisite knowledge, and therefore in effect virtually closed, because few do.

This is not to say that the House of Representatives is always and entirely out of touch with the world outside. It is to say, however, that the linkages between the citizenry and the House are more complex, variable, and tenuous than is generally realized.

The model of these linkages that most of us assume to be true looks something like Figure 7-1. Constituency preferences, filtered through the legislator's own policy views and his perceptions of constituency opinion, are ultimately translated into Yeas and Nays.[6] Each member engages in this activity independently. Some congressmen may place greater weight on their personal assessment of the merits of legislation (the Burkean "trustee" role) while others rely more heavily on preceived constituency views (a "delegate" role),[7] but the connection between the member and his district is direct and personal in either case.

The trouble with the direct-representation model is that it assumes far too high an information level on the part of both members of Congress and their constituents. It may be a fairly accurate picture of the process of representation when constituents *are* highly involved and the matter simple—emotionally charged, symbolic issues like flag-

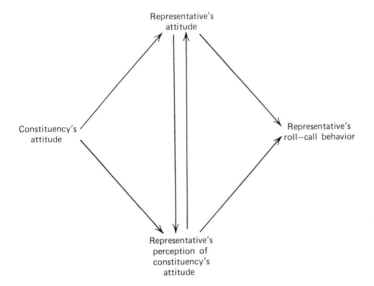

FIGURE 7-1   A direct-representation model

burning or school busing, for example. The decision processes of House experts, when dealing with issues falling within their area of special competence, may also bear some similarity to this process. But the vast bulk of matters—including most of the "important" ones—coming before the House are low-saliency issues for most congressmen and for most constituencies as well.

Figure 7-2 represents the "normal" voting situation. The linkage between the member and his constituents is indirect and attenuated. He has received no authoritative policy guidance from "back home" and, instead, makes up his mind on the basis of cues from his colleagues. The House experts—what we have called the initial cue-givers—have become the chamber's "windows on the world." These men and women are in more or less continuous contact with those persons and groups—bureaucrats, lobbyists, academic experts, media representatives, and others—who *are* interested and knowledgeable about the subject at hand.

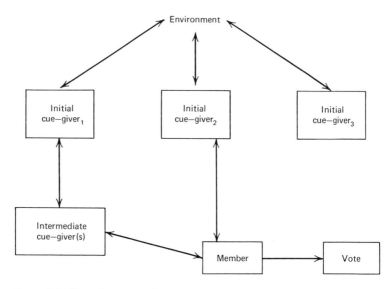

FIGURE 7-2   Normal representation.

This is, of course, a representative process of sorts. The House is not a mad Alice-in-Wonderland scene in which everyone looks to everyone else for cues with total disregard for the world outside. But *in the normal situation* at least, the linkages between the House member and those he was elected to represent are different from those we usually assume to exist. One indirect link, of course, is through the initial cue-givers. House "experts" are not just subject-matter specialists, but elective politicians too. Their colleagues are as interested in their judgments about the narrowly political consequences of a public policy as in their evaluation of its merits, if the two are even separable. How a given proposal will affect a cue-taker's constituents, what a cue-taker's constituency would conclude if it were paying attention—anticipations of this sort affect how *cue-givers* decide. Being well informed on a policy issue is rather fruitless if no other members look to them for cues. Members tend to look to those cue-givers whose policy evaluations will help them survive.

Elections are another link between congressmen and their constituents. A constituency that does not like a member can replace him. And a new member can develop a quite different cue-taking strategy from the former incumbent. The defeat of one of the House's premier cue-givers, although rare, can have massive effects on the cue-structure of the House, and hence on the content of public policy. While the outcomes of congressional elections do not often seem to hinge on policy matters, the policy *consequences* of elections can be substantial. But whether these changes result in more or less congruence between the member's voting on normal issues and the preponderant preferences of his constituents is an open question.

TECHNICAL COMPETENCE AND INSTITUTIONAL SURVIVAL

To ask why expertise is so important in the House is to ask why the House deals in matters of such complexity. Part of the answer is that government in the second half of the twentieth century is complicated. But this does not require a Congress that attempts to grapple with complexity, detail by detail.

Congress could fight a holding action with complexity, as many national legislatures have done, by delegating the details of governance to administrators and conerning itself only with broad policy matters. Such a course has often been advocated. "The hazard is that a body like Congress, when it gets into detail, *ceases to be itself,*" comments Arthur Macmahon.[8] In this view the function of legislatures is the consideration of broad policy questions; technical competence is not very important in dealing with them. Legislatures follow such advice at their peril for, in an increasingly complicated world, more and more policy conflicts involve details of implementation. As we saw in case of bank holding company legislation, the real conflicts may be over the means, not the ends, of proposed policies. It is these problems of means that usually require technical competence to resolve.

Coping with complexity has been the crowning achievement of Congress. Specialization and decision-making by cue-taking have been the means by which Congress has maintained decision-making autonomy in the twentieth century—in effect, the means by which it has survived as a *legislative* body. National legislatures unwilling or unable to adopt this expedient have withered into relative impotence, abdicating their policy-making role to bureaucracies and political executives.

The same may be said for the achievement of legislative competence and more or less rational collective decisions. Few institutions provide more power to the exceptionally competent member than does the House of Representatives. A Wilbur Mills on taxation or a George Mahon on defense appropriations probably knows more about his area than does any other member; within that realm, his power is awesome. The collective decisions of the House are disproportionately influenced by its most expert members. The cost of this happy state is a body that tends to be dominated by members whose views in their specialized domain may be far from representative of the House. By seeing the world through the eyes of its experts the House is a relatively closed system, and yet dependence on experts leads to technically competent decisions.

Whether responsiveness or competence is more to be valued we leave to the reader; we cannot have as much as we would like of both.

NOTES

1. Herbert A. Simon, *Models of Man* (New York: Wiley, 1967).

2. A. Campbell, P. Converse, W. Miller, and D. Stokes, *The American Voter* (New York: Wiley, 1960), see particularly Chapter 2.

3. The material on small-group decision-making in Congress is now too vast to be covered in a footnote, but of particular note—because they dovetail so nicely with our theory of cue-giving—is the work on policy subsystems in J. Leiper Freeman, *The Political Process: Executive Bureau-Legislative Committee Relations* (New York: Random House, 1955); and David Kovenock, "Influence in the U.S. House of Representatives: A Statistical Analysis of Communications." *American Politics Quarterly*, Vol. 1 (October 1973), pp. 407–464.

4. For a useful beginning see Sidney Verba and Norman Nie, *Participation in America: Political Democracy and Social Equality* (New York: Harper and Row, 1972), pp. 299–333.

5. The origin of our heading, minus the question mark, is from a study of the French National Assembly, Constantin Melnick and Nathan Leites, *The House Without Windows* (Evanston: Row, Peterson, 1958).

6. For the source of both Figure 7-1 and the explicit theory behind it see Warren Miller and Donald Stokes, "Constituency Influence in Congress," *American Political Science Review*, Vol. 57 (March 1963), pp. 45–56.

7. See John Wahlke, Heinz Eulau, William Buchanan, and Leroy Ferguson, *The Legislative System: Explorations in Legislative Behavior* (New York: Wiley, 1962).

8. Quoted in Roger Davidson and David Kovenock, "The Catfish and the Fisherman: Congress and Prescriptive Political Science," *American Behavioral Scientist,* Vol. 10 (1967), p. 25 (italics added).

INTERVIEW SCHEDULE WITH CODES AND RESPONSES

Most members seem to be active in a limited number of subjects.

Q1. In what areas of public policy are you most active and knowledgeable? (FRESHMEN: In what areas do you expect to be most active?)

ITEM (AND RESPONSES IN PARENTHESES)
Does R Consider Himself a "Specialist?"
(97)   1. Yes
 (3)   5. No

General Areas of Specialty
(11)   Agriculture
(11)   Appropriations
 (9)   Civil rights
(20)   Education
(20)   Foreign policy
(34)   General government

(3)   Health
(6)   Labor
(27) National security
(33) Resources and public works
(21) Taxes and economic policy
(9)   Transportation
(24) Welfare and urban affairs

Number of Specialty Areas
(3)   0. None
(48) 1. One
(41) 2. Two
(19) 3. Three
(8)   4. Four
(7)   5. Five

Relationship between Specialty and Committee Assignments
(3)   0. Inapplicable, does not specialize
(48) 1. Specialties fall exclusively within jurisdiction of present committee(s)
(6)   2. Specialties fall exclusively within jurisdiction of present and former committees
(41) 3. Specialties fall within jurisdiction of present committee(s) and others on which R has not served
(2)   4. Specialties do not fall within jurisdiction of present committee(s)

Q2. How is it that you came to specialize in these areas? (FRESHMEN: Why do you want to specialize in these areas?)

ITEM
Reasons for Specialty (up to four coded)
1.   Education and training
2.   Previous occupation
3.   Personal experience and background (exclusive of 1 and 2)

4. Service in other legislature
5. Constituency relevance
6. Committee responsibilities (used only if substantial interest developed after committee assignment)
7. Service in House (used for references to factors internal to the House)
0. Inapplicable
9. NA, noncodable

Q3. (OMIT FOR FRESHMEN) Now in _____ policy (policies) when do you usually make up your mind to give general support or opposition to pending legislation? (PROBE: That is, as soon as it is introduced, after the committee hearing or mark-up stage, after it has reached the floor, or when?)

ITEM
Earliest Decision Time
0. Inapplicable (freshman or does not specialize)
1. Before coming to Congress
2. Before introduced
3. At about the time legislation is introduced
4. During hearings
5. During committee deliberation and mark-up
6. During Floor debate
7. Just before voting
8. During voting on the Floor
9. NA, noncodable

Latest Decision Time (code as above)

Q4. Do you regularly communicate with other members about bills and resolutions in_____ policy (policies)?
Q4a. (IF YES) Who are they, that is, what type of member? We're not after names here unless you find it easier to answer the question that way.

ITEM

Does R Regularly Communicate with:

Committee Members?

- (0) 1. Chairman
- (0) 2. Ranking minority member
- (57) 3. Others
- (13) 4. Combination of first three
- (22) 5. No
- (5) 9. NA, noncodable
- (3) 0. Inapplicable

Party Leadership?

- (0) 1. Party leadership
- (0) 2. Party whip
- (3) 3. Conference, policy committee, or task forces
- (3) 4. "The Leadership"
- (85) 5. No
- (6) 9. NA, noncodable
- (3) 0. Inapplicable

Members of State Delegation?

- (12) 1. Yes
- (78) 5. No
- (6) 9. NA, noncodable
- (4) 0. Inapplicable

Members of Sociolegislative Group?

- (8) 1. Democratic Study Group
- (1) 2. Wednesday Group
- (0) 3. SOS
- (3) 4. Class Groups
- (0) 6. Chowder and Marching Society
- (3) 7. Other
- (4) 8. Combination
- (72) 5. No

(6)   9.   NA, noncodable
(3)   0.   Inapplicable

Others?
     (4)   1.   All members (by letter)
     (9)   2.   Those with same views
    (24)   3.   Others (unspecified)
    (11)   4.   Noncommittee members (general)
    (44)   5.   No
     (5)   9.   NA, noncodable
     (3)   0.   Inapplicable

Q4b.   Do they usually contact you, or do you usually seek them out?

ITEM
Direction of Communication
     (2)   1.   They contact R
     (5)   2.   R contacts them
    (78)   3.   Mutual contact
    (11)   9.   NA, noncodable
     (4)   0.   Inapplicable

Q4c.   When does this usually happen? (PROBE: That is, at what
       stage in the legislative process?

ITEM
Earliest Communication
0.   Inapplicable (freshman or does not specialize or communi-
     cate)
1.   Before coming to Congress
2.   Before introduced
3.   At about the time legislation is introduced
4.   During hearings
5.   During committee deliberations and mark-up
6.   During floor debate

7. Just before voting
8. During voting on the floor
9. NA, noncodable

Latest Communication (Code as above)

Now we'd like you to generalize about *all* the measures you are expected to vote on each session, not just those in your area of specialty.

Q5. Does your personal staff ever study pieces of pending legislation and relevant committee documents and give you a memorandum or briefing on them? (IF YES) Q5a. About how often?

ITEM
Staff Legislative Assistance
- (28) 1. *No, never* (doesn't work, not enough people, not right people, etc.)
- (36) 2. *Occasionally* and *intermittently* (important bills, when interns available, etc.)
- (31) 3. *Frequently* and *regularly* (staff prepares material on all bills mentioned in whip notices each week, etc.)
- (0) 5. *Always* on all bills
- (5) 9. NA, noncodable

Q6. And how often are you able personally to read the bill or committee report before you cast your vote on the floor?

ITEM
R Reads Committee Reports and/or Bills
- (4) 1. Never
- (44) 2. Occasionally and intermittently
- (38) 3. Frequently and regularly
- (3) 5. Always on all bills
- (11) 9. NA, noncodable (includes "I try to read report.")
- (0) 0. Inapplicable

Conditions under which R Reads Bill
(11)   1.   Never
 (4)   2.   Only if committee report unclear
 (1)   3.   Only if minority views in report
 (2)   4.   Only if bill is short
 (3)   5.   Only if bill is important
 (1)   6.   Always on important bills
 (3)   7.   Always on all bills
(73)   9.   NA, noncodable
 (2)   0.   Inapplicable

Q7.   During an average day, about how much time are you able to
      spend studying legislation?

ITEM
All legislative Study
 (0)   1.   None
 (0)   2.   Thirty minutes or less
 (4)   3.   Thirty minutes to an hour
 (7)   4.   One to two hours
(17)   5.   Two to four hours
 (9)   6.   More than four hours
(44)   8.   Noncodable response
(19)   9.   NA, DK
 (0)   0.   Inapplicable (doesn't specialize)

Q7a. And how much of this time is generally devoted to study out-
      side of your area of legislative specialization?

ITEM
Legislative Study outside of specialty
 (2)   1.   None
(21)   2.   Thirty minutes or less
(11)   3.   Thirty minutes to an hour
 (7)   4.   One to two hours

(1) 5. Two to four hours
(0) 6. More than four hours
(36) 8. Noncodable response
(19) 9. NA, DK
(3) 0. Inapplicable (doesn't specialize)

Q8. How often do you think that most of your constituents know or care how you can vote on specific bills? (IF NECESSARY) Q8a. How often are you *confident* that you know what most of your constituents want you to do on an issue *before* you must cast a public vote on it?

ITEM
How Often Do R's Constituents Know?
(0) 1. Never
(63) 2. Seldom (1–25% of the votes)
(16) 3. Frequently (25–75% of the votes)
(1) 4. Almost always (75% +)
(9) 8. Noncodable
(11) 9. NA, DK

Types of Issues and Circumstances when Constituents are Aware of R's Votes on Specific Bills
Only "Emotional" Issues (e.g., gun control, Congressional salaries, etc.)
(17) 1. Yes
(80) 5. No mention
(3) 0. Inapplicable

Only on Issues of Direct Personal Concern to Constituents
(32) 1. Yes
(65) 5. No mention
(3) 0. Inapplicable

Only on Controversial Bills of National Importance
(13) 1. Yes

(84)   5.   No mention
 (3)   0.   Inapplicable

Only on Issues Covered by the Local Press and TV
(21)   1.   Yes
(76)   5.   No Mention
 (3)   0.   Inapplicable

Only around Election Time and during Campaigns
(10)   1.   Yes
(87)   5.   No mention
 (3)   0.   Inapplicable

Now we'd like you to try to generalize again, this time about the situation when the member and his staff have not studied the measure and when the interests of the member's constituents are not felt to be particularly involved.

Q9.   How often does this situation occur for the typical member?

ITEM
Frequency of Low-Information Situation for *Typical Member*
 (0)   1.   Never
(12)   2.   Seldom (1–25%)
(65)   3.   Frequently (25–75%)
 (3)   4.   Almost always (75% +)
(10)   8.   Noncodable
(10)   9.   NA, DK

Q10.   What about you? (Reference to Q9)

ITEM
Frequency of Low-Information Situation for R
 (0)   1.   Never
(19)   2.   Seldom

(62) 3. Frequently
 (4) 4. Almost always
(10) 8. Noncodable
 (5) 9. NA, DK

Q11. When this situation occurs and you must cast a Floor vote but know very little about the issue involved, what do you do?

Q12. In this situation do you regularly communicate with other members? (IF YES) Q12a. Who are they, that is, what type of member? Q12b. Do you usually seek out these members or do they usually contact you?

ITEM
R Takes Cues
(96) 1. Yes
 (4) 5. No

Q12c. When does this usually happen?

Q13. (IF NECESSARY: Again, in this situation when do you usually make up your mind to give general support or opposition to pending legislation?)

ITEM
Earliest Time of Decision Mentioned
0. Inapplicable (freshman or does not specialize)
1. Before coming to Congress
2. Before introduced
3. At about the time legislation is introduced
4. During hearings
5. During committee deliberations and mark-up
6. During floor debate
7. Just before voting
8. During voting on the floor
9. NA, noncodable

Latest Time of Decision Mentioned (Code as above)

Q14.   Now I'd like to ask you a hypothetical question. Suppose you
        had to cast a roll-call vote and could know only the position of
        three of the people or groups on this list. (HAND R FLASH
        CARD WITH LIST OF TEN CUE-GIVERS.) Which three
        would you want to know? (GET RANK 1, 2, 3.)

        ITEM
        First Choice (if no group is mentioned, code as blank)
        (27)   0.   The majority of R's state party delegation
         (6)   1.   The majority of R's party
        (10)   2.   The president
        (14)   3.   The Democratic Study Group
         (0)   4.   The Wednesday Group
         (2)   5.   The "Conservative Coalition"
        (13)   6.   The chairman of the reporting committee
         (6)   7.   The ranking minority member of the reporting
                    committee
         (1)   8.   The majority of all members
         (8)   9.   The leadership of R's party

        Second Choice
        Third Choice

Q15.   Are there other individuals or groups whose position you'd
        rather know than any of the three just mentioned?

        ITEM
        Are There Additional Sources?
        (43)   1.   Yes
        (39)   5.   No
        (18)   9.   Noncodable, NA

Additional Sources Mentioned

(12) 1. Someone on the committee, but not the chairman or ranking member

(1) 2. R's wife

(10) 3. Lobbies

(10) 4. Outstanding individuals in the House

(4) 5. Policy committee

(3) 6. Staff, doorkeeper

(2) 7. Another sociolegislative group

(1) 8. Senator

(57) 9. NA, DK, inapplicable, noncodable

Q16. Do you see a great deal of the other members from _____ (STATE)?

ITEM

Sees Members of Delegation?

(28) 1. Yes—General

(27) 2. Yes—Regular, formal meetings

(29) 3. Yes—informal, on Floor, at social occasions, etc.

(11) 5. No

(1) 8. Inapplicable—one-man delegation

(4) 9. NA, DK, noncodable

Q16a. Is this the entire delegation or just the _____ (PARTY)?

Q16b. Is that all of them or just some of them?

ITEM

Who Meets?

(21) 1. Entire delegation

(46) 2. Entire party delegation

(10) 3. Portion of party delegation

(5) 4. Portion of delegation (across party lines)

(8) 0. Inapplicable

(10) 9. NA, DK

If Only Portion of Delegation, Basis of Discrimination
(2) 1. Age/tenure (e.g., young versus old)
(1) 2. Ideology
(7) 3. Geography
(4) 4. Personal friendship
(76) 0. Inapplicable
(10) 9. NA, DK

Q17. (IF NOT ALREADY ANSWERED) How would you say
      that this amount of communication compares with that of other
      delegations that you are familiar with?

      ITEM
      Relative Interaction
      (31) 1. More
      (19) 2. About the same
      (24) 3. Less
       (1) 0. Inapplicable

Q18. Most delegations vote together rather frequently. How would
      you account for this?
      ITEM
      Primary Reason
      (12) 1. Similar type of men (background and philosophy)
      (34) 2. Similar constituencies
      (17) 3. Personal interaction within delegation (friendship,
               caucuses, etc.)
       (6) 4. "Defensive advantage," protective coloration
       (7) 5. Party discipline
       (1) 6. Interest in state-wide office
      (22) 9. NA, DK, noncodable
       (1) 0. Inapplicable

      Other Reasons (Code as above)
      Other Reasons (Code as above)

Q19. Some members say that their party leaders in the House put

too much "pressure" on them; others feel that the leaders
don't provide enough guidance. How do you feel?

ITEM
Party Leadership
  (5) 1. Too much
(57) 3. About right
(25) 5. Not enough
  (8) 9. NA, DK, noncodable
  (5) 0. Inapplicable (freshman)

Q20. What about the President and his staff? (Reference to Q19)

ITEM
Presidential Leadership
  (8) 1. Too much
(51) 3. About right
(10) 5. Not enough
(24) 9. NA, DK, noncodable
  (7) 0. Inapplicable (freshman)

Q21. How often would you say that bills have sufficient ideological
flavor that your voting decision can be made largely on the
basis of ideology?

ITEM
How Often?
  (8) 1. Never
(38) 2. Seldom (1–25%)
(29) 3. Frequently (25–75%)
  (4) 4. Almost always (75% +)
  (5) 5. Always
(21) 9. NA, DK, noncodable

Q22. What do you see as the most powerful groups or interests in
your district?

ITEM
Categories of Perception of Groups in the District

Party
(20)   1.   Democratic district
(10)   2.   Republican district
 (6)   3.   Independent, ticket-splitting, unpredictable
 (6)   4.   Mixed
(50)   5.   No mention
 (8)   9.   NA, DK, noncodable

Ideology
 (2)   1.   Liberal
 (3)   2.   Moderate, middle of the road
(12)   3.   Conservative
(12)   4.   Mixed
(63)   5.   No mention
 (8)   9.   NA, DK, noncodable

Class Composition
 (4)   1.   Working class
 (3)   2.   Middle class
 (4)   3.   Upper-middle, upper class
(18)   4.   Mixed
(63)   5.   No mention
 (8)   9.   NA, DK, noncodable

Type of Communities
 (6)   1.   Urban
 (6)   2.   Rural
(11)   3.   Suburban
(24)   4.   Mixed
(45)   5.   No mention
 (8)   9.   NA, DK, Noncodable

Organized Interest Groups
(13) 0. None
 (5) 1. One
(15) 2. Two
(20) 3. Three
(16) 4. Four
(15) 5. Five
 (2) 6. Six
 (1) 7. Seven
 (6) 8. Eight
 (7) 9. NA, DK

Private Nonpolitical Organizations (e.g., specific companies, universities, churches, newspapers, etc.)
(25) 1. Yes
(67) 5. No mention
 (8) 9. NA, DK, inapplicable

Number of Categories R Mentions
 (5) 0. None
(10) 1. One
(27) 2. Two
(24) 3. Three
(20) 4. Four
 (3) 5. Five
 (3) 6. Six
 (8) 9. NA, DK

Q23. Some members feel pretty certain that they will be reelected while others feel very insecure in their seats? What about you?

ITEM
R's Subjective Security
 (2) 1. Highly insecure
(18) 2. Insecure

(13)   3.   Secure from everything but national landslides or redistricting
(55)   4.   Secure
(12)   9.   NA, DK, noncodable

Q24.   Some members seem to be concerned about winning the approval and respect of their colleagues in the House. Other members don't seem to think the approval and respect of their colleagues is that important. What do you think?

ITEM
How Important Is Approval and Respect?
 (8)   1.   Not important
(27)   2.   Important with reservations (don't overdo, constituents more important, etc.)
(56)   3.   Very important
 (9)   9.   NA, DK, noncodable

APPENDIX B

SAMPLING AND INTERVIEWING TECHNIQUES

The sampling universe for the interview portion of this study included all members of the House in March 1969, except the Speaker, Majority Leader, Minority Leader, Majority Whip, Minority Whip and chairmen of standing committees. With four seats vacant at the time of the interviewing program, that left 405 members in the universe.

The nonleader universe differs from the House in two respects. Twenty-nine of the 31 excluded leaders were Democrats, and all 31 were high in the seniority rankings. The universe is thus slightly more Republican and slightly less senior than the House. (But chance, not intent, is responsible for the 50-50 partisan split of the *sample*.)

Members were drawn from the universe by random assignment of ranks. The first 100 members on the rank list were contacted. Each time that it became clear that one of the original 100 could not be interviewed, contact was initated with the highest ranked remaining member. In all, 111 members were contacted, resulting in 100 completed interviews.

The 11 nonrespondents are almost evenly split between parties, five

Democrats and 6 Republicans. They are regionally diverse and somewhat more senior than the House norm, but not dramatically so. Roughly three categories of explanation account for our failure to obtain interviews from them.

Some of the 11 were simply unavailable. Two of them were seeking higher office and were virtually never in Washington. Two suffered prolonged illnesses during the interviewing period.

Some nonresponse may be explained by the difficulty of scheduling interviews for exceptionally busy members. Five of the 11 nonrespondents served on particularly time-consuming exclusive committees. Finally, some members are simply unwilling to grant academic interviews. It is difficult to draw the line between the "too busy" and the "unwilling," so it is not clear how many nonresponses should be in each category.

Taken as a whole, response was good. Some 90 percent of all members contacted granted interviews. Of those for whom it was reasonably possible to grant interviews, a smaller group, the proportion doing so is probably on the order of 95 percent.

Our interviewing technique was an attempt to strike a compromise between the conflicting needs of structure and comparability on the one hand, and rapport and candor on the other. The interview schedule of Appendix A is structured, but it was administered as if it were unstructured. No printed interview schedule was used. Questions were phrased conversationally, were sometimes asked out of order, and were even sometimes redesigned in midinterview as probes to follow up on earlier member comments. When the demands of structure conflicted with the requisites of candor, more often than not the conflict was resolved in favor of the latter.

APPENDIX C

SOME TECHNICAL COMMENTS ON THE COMPUTER SIMULATION

The LEARN program described in Chapter 6 consists of 437 PL/1 statements. It was designed to run on an IBM 360/75 computing system. Although its design is system-free, its language and storage requirements combine to restrict it to the larger versions of the 360 system.

Principal program requirements are immense core storage and great speed. Substantial storage is required because at one point a matrix of all roll-call votes cast by all congressmen for a year must be stored. (The program logic is capable of sequential processing of all votes in an entire Congress, not just in a year, but the large numbers of roll-call votes in recent Congresses have made that feat too demanding of computer facilities.) Great speed is required because the program must define nearly all of the possible cues on each vote individually for each of the 435 members. That task is conceptually easy but enormously demanding of the computer.

The extraordinary flexibility of PL/1 proved to be not merely convenient, but necessary to enable LEARN to run without overwhelming the capabilities of even the largest available computing systems. The program requires storage to contain several very large matrices, one of which reaches a limit of 245 by 442 (or about 108,000 bytes) for the number of votes cast in one year by all members. Simulating that number of votes involves billions of discrete steps, pushing time requirements to the point of great expense and inconvenience. The simultaneous strain on both time and storage capacity meant that neither space nor speed could be significantly sacrificed to optimize the other.

PL/1 allows the programmer great latitude in defining internal representation and storage. That proved useful in a number of ways. The largest matrices were stored in bytes of minimal size [Decimal Fixed (1)]. Segregated BEGIN BLOCKS allowed the use of the same storage space for different matrices at different points in the program. In the first block the "Votes by Members" matrix (in the Inter-University Consortium for Political Research Historical Data Archive format) is read and stored, occupying almost all available storage space. It is then inverted into a "Members by Votes" matrix and written on a slow-core storage device. At the end of the block all that storage space is freed up for other uses, and the variable "Vote" is redefined as a unidimensional array of length equal to the number of members in the House.

Since the "Vote" matrix is never again present in core—only one vote at a time is present—the "forgetting" mechanism of the 50-vote memory feature caused new complications. To delete for each member the impact of the $i - 50$th vote we faced the choice of a costly replication of the situation of that vote or of somehow storing the information. Since each member responds in the model to nine cue-givers, the storage matrix would have had to be 9 by 50 by 442 or, at minimum, nearly 200,000 bytes. That space was not available, nor could we have afforded the costs in time of retrieving these data from external storage devices.

The PL/1 bit-string capacity solved this problem. Bit strings can be strung together in varying lengths to achieve optimal economy of core storage. Two binary bits were required to code the requisite memory data for each cue-giver for each vote for each member. One recorded whether or not the cue was available and the member voting (CAMV) and one whether the member in question voted with the cue-giver (VWC). All of this information was contained in strings of 900 bits (18 bits for each of 50 votes) for each of 442 members. The bit strings were manipulated by adding on at one end and "pushing down" the string to remove the 18 bits for vote $i - 50$ from the other.

The second block contains all of the essential logic of the simulation. It is organized with a single loop that directs the chronological processing of roll calls and contains the logic for "learning" and "forgetting" cue-responses patterns, employing massive bit strings to represent "memory." It measures past cue-response patterns, evaluates current positions of cue-givers, and predicts each member's vote.

The final block monitors the predictive success and failure of the simulation, by member and by roll call, and outputs a variety of housekeeping and accounting information.

INDEX

Middlesex County College Library

3 9320 00028345 4

JK
1447
M38
Y43

Matthews

Yeas and nays: normal
decision-making in the
U. S. House of...

Date Due

**Middlesex County
College Library**

PRINTED IN U.S.A.